Applied Psychology
for Law Enforcement
and Correction Officers

Applied Psychology for Law Enforcement and Correction Officers

Robert J. Wicks

Training Consultant for
Curriculum Development
Center for Correctional Training
Department of Correction
City of New York

Adjunct Instructor
Institute of Criminal Justice
St. John's University
St. Vincent's College

McGRAW-HILL BOOK COMPANY

New York   Kuala Lumpur   Panama
St. Louis   London   Rio de Janeiro
San Francisco   Mexico   Singapore
Düsseldorf   Montreal   Sydney
Johannesburg   New Delhi   Toronto

ABOUT THE AUTHOR

Robert J. Wicks has directed correctional mental health treatment programs both in the United States and overseas. He has written articles in the field and has coauthored several applied psychology texts. Before coming to New York, the author was a lecturer on Human Behavior, in the Law Enforcement Division, Department of Community Colleges, North Carolina.

Currently he is Training Consultant for Curriculum Development, Center for Correctional Training, Department of Correction, New York City; and adjunct instructor at St. John's University.

Library of Congress Cataloging in Publication Data

Wicks, Robert J

    Applied psychology for law enforcement and correction officers.

    Bibliography: p.
    1. Psychology. 2. Interviewing in law enforcement. 3. Law enforcement. 4. Corrections. I. Title.
[DNLM: 1. Criminal psychology. HV 6080 W637a 1974]
BF 131.W68 363.2′ 01′9 73-1706
ISBN 0-07-070103-2

The editors for this book were Ardelle Cleverdon and Suzanne Kistler, the designer was Marsha Cohen, and its production was supervised by Patricia Ollague. It was set in Century by Port City Press Inc.

It was printed and bound by R. R. Donnelley & Sons Company.

Applied Psychology for Law Enforcement and Correction Officers

1 2 3 4 5 6 7 8 9 0 DODO 7 9 8 7 6 5 4

For My Wife, Michaele

Contents

Preface

Law enforcement officers are in constant daily contact with all types of individuals. Often those they deal with are under great emotional stress, which causes them to act in a violent or otherwise unusual manner. In such situations—that is, when people behave abnormally—the officer must be able to react professionally.

Professionalism results from experience, but not from experience alone. Education is also an essential element. And in recognition of the need for education, law enforcement agencies throughout the nation are raising the standards for their applicants. In addition, they are encouraging the present members of their forces to return to school during their off-duty hours and to read professional books in the field.

This book, created as a text for a course given in the police science field, is specifically written to aid the officer in his pursuit of further education. It is designed to provide basic theoretical and practical psychological information.

There are four sections in this text: general psychology, abnormal psychology, psychology of interviewing and interrogation, and psychology in law enforcement.

The first section on general psychology presents a brief introduction to the field of psychology, gives some basic tenets, and notes how they apply to the reader.

A section on abnormal psychology is included to give the reader a view of the different types of mental illness. The chapters in this area deal with neurosis, psychosis, and character disorders. Special treatment is given to alcoholism and drug addiction.

The two chapters devoted to techniques in interviewing and interrogation are designed to present a number of principles which can be employed in the interview of a subordinate, witness, prisoner, or parolee, as well as during the interrogation of a suspect.

The final section covers areas in which psychology is being used in law enforcement and corrections. Chapters on correctional psychology, traffic safety, crowd control, and community relations comprise this area of the book.

The main objectives of this text are to:

1. Introduce the reader to general psychology, abnormal psychology, and the psychology of interviewing and interrogation so that he may understand some *basic* principles in these areas and be motivated to take courses in them sometime in the future.

2. Assist the reader to understand more fully his own actions and those of others.

3. Inform the reader of the part psychology plays in the field of law enforcement and corrections.

Whether the reader uses this book as a text for a course or as part of a program of reading professional material, it is hoped that it will aid him in one of the most difficult and important specialties today—law enforcement.

—*Robert J. Wicks*

Acknowledgments

For permission to utilize copyrighted material I wish to thank Smith, Kline & French Laboratories, the Christopher D. Smithers Foundation, A.A. World Services, and the McGraw-Hill Book Company.

For their encouragement, advice, and support, I would also like to express my appreciation to Drs. William Louy and John Wright, Phillip D. Sumner, Roland J. Howard, and Ralph Roper.

I am also grateful to Sheila Lanza, who typed the manuscript, and whose patience and fine work helped immeasurably.

Above all though, for her tireless assistance, I wish to thank my wife, Michaele. Without her, the project would probably never have reached completion.

Applied Psychology
for Law Enforcement
and Correction Officers

section one

General Psychology

chapter one

Introduction
to Personality
and Psychology

The psychology of human relations is an expanding field of study. Today, everyone appears to have some knowledge in this area. Moreover, it is even becoming a requirement in certain professions to be well versed in psychology in order to be more adept in dealing with individuals and groups. It is logical that law enforcement should move in this direction because of the many and varied types of people that its officers come in contact with on a daily basis.

WHAT IS PERSONALITY?

One of the main goals of the study of human relations is an understanding of how to interact with others. To accomplish this, one should be able to understand more clearly why a person responds in the way he does. In this pursuit it would be helpful to know first of all what personality is and how it develops.

Everyone has a view of himself and a view of the world. It is *constant* and *unique*. This means that an individual sees himself differently from the way that others view him, regardless of whether they like him or not. As a result, his particular view of himself leads to his viewing the world in a unique way; and in turn, how he views himself and the world leads up to the way he will act or respond toward it. In other words, if he views the world as a hostile, threatening place, it is likely that he will strike out against it. If he

3

looks upon himself as a terrible person, he's not going to try to utilize his potential because he will be convinced that he has none. In addition, as noted above, this outlook is relatively constant since people change very little from day to day. One can then define personality as *the constant, unique way a person views himself and the world.* And so, with this definition as a frame of reference, the reader can now move on to the subject of how personality develops.

HOW DOES A PERSONALITY DEVELOP?

Personality depends on two factors: *body equipment* and *environment.* Body equipment is the entire physical material (brain, central nervous system, etc.) with which one is endowed at birth. This material is influenced by three elements:

1. Heredity
2. Prenatal environment
3. Birth injuries

Heredity has a direct influence on body equipment. It is a process which establishes a kind of blueprint for those body parts which are to develop and grow. On the other hand, prenatal environment and birth injuries have more of an indirect bearing.

By "prenatal environment," it is not suggested that if a mother listens to classical music during pregnancy, her child will be born with an appreciation of this type of music. Rather, prenatal environment refers to occurrences by which the mother is physically affected. For example, if the mother is a narcotic addict, there is a good chance that the child could be born with withdrawal symptoms. And as far as the influence of birth injuries on body equipment is concerned, it is obvious that any mishap during delivery could result in the baby's being handicapped.

Having looked at the factors involved in what the individual has to work with at birth, we realize that men are not all created equal. In fact, *body equipment has a great bearing on man's potential.* If a person has no feet, his potential as a baseball player is naturally lower than someone who has both feet. Someone who is 7 feet tall should be able to play a better game of basketball than someone who at maturity is 5 feet 1 inch. Yet, as the reader knows, there are average-sized individuals who can actually play a better game of basketball than people who tower over them. This is where the second factor that affects personality and ability comes in—environment.

Environment in this context, however, does not mean trees and buildings but refers to the persons who are significant in each individual's life. Parents, teachers, siblings, and peers are good examples of those who make up the "people environment" that affects a human being's development.

And of all the individuals society can tag as significant, the person acting as mother is probably the one who has the most impact on a child's formation. The baby looks on the mother as the person who provides satisfaction of his needs and relief of pain. Therefore the child tries to please her so that he will not be cut off. The mother thus has the power to form the child's personality or self-concept by responding in a positive way to the behavior which she finds desirable (smiling, for example) and negatively to the behavior which she doesn't like in the child (crying, bed-wetting). Consequently, through the use of trial and error with his mother and other significant persons, the child learns moral and social behavior—what he should do and how he should act. This is why the 5-foot boy might be able to play basketball better than one who is 7 feet tall. If the 7-foot boy never bothered with the game because his father or his friends didn't think it was the thing to do, his lack of motivation and experience would make him inferior in a basketball game to someone who had been encouraged (reinforced) to play it. Therefore, through an examination of the influence of the environment on personality, two more facts come to light.

1. One's view of oneself and the world is *learned* from the important persons in one's life.
2. A person's environment determines how close he will come to reaching his potential.

So one can see that even though people are not equal at birth, the really important determinant of individual differences is the result of what is learned from the significant persons (environment) in one's life, not what an individual has to work with when he is born (body equipment).

UNDERSTANDING THE CONCEPT OF PERSONALITY

Realizing how one's personality has been formed provides an opportunity to reflect on how it affects his present view of life. In addition, a realization of the fact that those one deals with are working from a particular framework, a unique self-concept, should cause one to have greater respect for their right to be different and possibly to have a greater tolerance of their views. With this understanding it is possible to come to a better knowledge of oneself and those with whom one comes into contact each day.

The psychology of personality is worthy of particular attention. Moreover, a deeper understanding of psychological principles and their application to the field of law enforcement would indeed be of assistance to police officers. It will be helpful, then, to take a closer look at psychology.

WHAT IS PSYCHOLOGY?

Psychology is *the science of behavior*.[1] Though simply stated here, this definition is the result of a long period of development and formation in the field. Since it is now accepted by a majority of psychologists that the two words *science* and *behavior* should be included in a description of the field, the above definition might even be considered a major breakthrough. The reason this seems so is that psychology from its beginning until quite recently was defined in such ways as "the art of consciousness" or "the study of the mind." These definitions lacked the objectivity necessary for psychology if it were to be classified as a science. As a science, its research methods should result in information which is *verifiable* and *able to be communicated*, so the data produced would not be built on a foundation of opinions and guesses but on agreed-upon observations. This was, and is, desirable.

Another part of the description of psychology is the word *behavior*. To the psychologist, behavior is *the observable actions of the organism*. The emphasis here is on the *actions* of an organism because, as a scientist, the psychologist is more interested in actions and reactions which can be seen and verified than in concepts which cannot be directly verified. Therefore, the definition briefly examined above, though simple to remember, has deeper implications to those who study psychology.

FALSE BELIEFS AND COMMON SENSE

Now that we have looked at the definition of psychology, it is appropriate to view some common errors made concerning the

[1] See Clifford T. Morgan, *Introduction to Psychology*, McGraw-Hill, New York, 1961, p. 2; Cameron Fincher, *A Preface to Psychology*, Harper & Row, New York, 1964, p. 18; James O. Whittaker, *Introduction to Psychology*, Saunders, Philadelphia, 1966, p. 582.

science of behavior and those who practice in the field. These errors are mentioned here in order to demonstrate that what often appears to be widely accepted as fact (common sense) is actually false.

Three theories which are untrue, though still accepted by some people today, are *numerology*, *palmistry*, and *phrenology*. Each of these claims the ability to predict events and conditions with accuracy (numerology by the number of letters in one's name, palmistry by studying the palm of the hand, and phrenology by examining the conformation of the skull). These claims when tested are found to have no factual basis at all, and yet today a number of persons are still employing these so-called useful methods with gullible individuals. Fortunately, their use is diminishing.

These theories are probably considered invalid by most people today. However, there are a number of false statements which many still believe, such as:

1. *Blind persons are born with a highly developed sense of touch and specially sensitive hearing.* This erroneous claim is part of a belief that nature compensates for a deficiency in one sense with an increased acuteness in another sense. Now it is true that most blind persons observed probably do have well-developed senses of hearing and touch, but this is not innate (possessed from birth) but rather developed through *learning*.

2. *You can learn while you're asleep, through the aid of a phonograph or tape recorder.* This is false, for one cannot learn while really (deeply) asleep; quite simply, one cannot hear what is being broadcasted. Whatever is claimed to be learned is, in actual fact, the result of what is heard before the individual is fully asleep.

3. *Psychologists can "psychoanalyze" an individual by sitting down with him for a short session.* This statement contains two false elements. One, psychoanalysts are specially trained psychiatrists and social scientists; not every psychologist is a psychoanalyst—as a matter of fact, very few are. Also, psychoanalysis is an extremely lengthy process, often taking years. Moreover, this point brings us to another similar misconception, namely, that a psychologist can quickly and easily understand a person's whole personality, as if it were an open book. It is not unusual for a psychologist upon meeting someone socially to hear the person say in jest, "I hope you're not going to psych me out," with a nervous laugh and a show of uneasiness. No expert on human behavior, even if he were the Sherlock Holmes of psychology, could deduce the inner secrets of another person from brief encounters.

These examples are sufficient to demonstrate that what often passes for a commonsense conclusion concerning behavior is not always true, and that the science of behavior has as one of its goals the elimination of widespread misconceptions that are now considered valid. One of the responsibilities of the student of psychology is to further advance his knowledge so that he can replace myths with facts and learn to recognize errors made by others concerning this science.

WHAT IS THE DIFFERENCE BETWEEN PSYCHOLOGY, PSYCHIATRY, AND PSYCHOANALYSIS?

To conclude this chapter aptly while taking into account what has been covered thus far, there are two more general areas in which to delve. First, a description will be provided of the professional background and area of specialization of psychiatrists, psychologists, and psychoanalysts so that they can be distinguished from one another; finally, a survey of the categories of psychology will be listed and discussed in order to give a better overall view of what psychology covers.

Since this is a book on psychology, it is only fitting that the reader understand who a psychologist is and what he does. A psychologist has a B.A. or B.S. degree, which takes four years to acquire, an M.A. or M.S. degree requiring another year, and in most areas a Ph.D., which takes two to three additional years of college. He is primarily a member of the academic community, because his training is centered at a university (though as a clinical psychologist he would also be required in most cases to work as an intern in a psychiatric hospital for a year). His main duties could include teaching, psychotherapy, research, and psychological testing, depending upon the field of psychology in which he is involved (an experimental psychologist would not be involved in psychotherapy, whereas a clinical psychologist probably would). A psychologist is also often called in as a consultant to industrial, religious, and political organizations, educational institutions, and fields such as law enforcement and nursing. As you can see, the psychologist's work is diversified.

A psychiatrist, on the other hand, has a B.S. degree and also an M.D. professional degree, which takes four years of additional study followed by an internship and residency (usually three years) in a psychiatric hospital. As far as the psychiatrist's duties are concerned, he is usually involved in the following areas: administration of a psychiatric hospital or agency, psychotherapy, teaching, and research.

To elaborate this outline of the duties which psychologists and psychiatrists normally perform, it might help to emphasize here that the psychologist often does testing, but the psychiatrist rarely does. Also, a psychiatrist, as a medical doctor, is the one who would usually be named as administrator of a psychiatric hospital or mental institution. In addition, the psychiatrist can prescribe drugs, while the psychologist cannot. In other words, the important thing to remember in distinguishing the psychologist (who has a Ph.D.) from the psychiatrist (who has an M.D.) is that *the psychiatrist is a medical doctor*. If you can recall this fact, the confusion in referring to these two professionals will be eliminated.

Psychoanalysts are in yet another category, though not completely divorced from either psychology or psychiatry. A psychoanalyst is usually a psychiatrist, but psychologists and social workers can become *lay* psychoanalysts. The requirements for a qualified individual to attain this title are that he must attend an institution of training in psychoanalysis (which is based on the principles set forth by Freud and his followers) and also that he be analyzed himself. To get a picture of this person in your mind you need only think of the analyst who is sitting by a couch on which his patient is lying—this scene has been popularized by books and movies for years. His role is primarily one of practicing a deep form of psychotherapy (psychoanalysis or analysis) in which he is often seeking to accomplish a major change in the personality makeup of his patient. It is a task that could take months or years—or that might perhaps never end.

FIELDS OF PSYCHOLOGY

As noted before, psychologists can be involved in doing research, having a therapy practice, and teaching. These efforts are further subdivided according to an interest or interests in some area of emphasis in psychology's diversified fields. The following list mentions ten areas and gives brief descriptions of each.

1. *Clinical Psychology* This area deals with the emotional troubles of individuals by employing techniques such as psychotherapy, behavior therapy, and psychological testing in an effort to alleviate the person's problem. In addition, this field concerns itself with research on how to improve the methods being used.
2. *Experimental Psychology* Specialists in this field are involved in psychological research (learning, sensation, problem solving).
3. *Physiological Psychology* Individuals in this area of interest are physio-

logically oriented researchers and are concerned with muscular activity, localization of the memory in the brain, etc.

4. *Educational Psychology* As might be surmised from the title, this is an area in which psychology is applied to education. Typical questions are: How can one increase the motivation of the student? Does the shape of the classroom have an impact on studying?

5. *Social Psychology* Social conditions, prejudices, public opinion polls, and so on—all these topics interest the social psychologist.

6. *Industrial Psychology* This is psychology applied to industry in which the aim is to help increase production and sales. An example of this would be a study by a psychologist on what type of commercial appeals to a housewife in the Midwest.

7. *Psychological Testing* The creation, administration, and evaluation of tests and techniques of measurement form this branch of study.

8. *Developmental Psychology* A main interest of this area is the effect of heredity and environment on children.

9. *Abnormal Psychology* This category is of course concerned with the causes, prevention, and treatment of mental illnesses.

10. *Comparative Psychology* Here the psychologist deals with comparisons between different species of animals, concentrating on the similarities and differences in behavior.

WHAT WAS COVERED IN THIS CHAPTER

This chapter has provided a brief introduction to psychology and personality. Psychology was defined as the science of behavior, and personality as the constant, unique way in which a person views himself and the world. It was also noted that heredity and birth injuries determine a person's potential, whereas environment determines how close he will come to actualizing it.

In addition, behavior was defined as the observable actions of an organism, and the validity of some commonsense observations was challenged. The chapter concluded with an examination of the differences between a psychologist, who has a Ph.D., and a psychiatrist, who has an M.D. and is therefore permitted to prescribe drugs.

The ten fields of psychology were listed and briefly described at the end of the chapter. These included clinical, abnormal, experimental, physiological, educational, social, developmental, industrial, and comparative psychology, and psychological testing.

All of the foregoing information was provided so that the reader would have a better understanding of what is implied by the term psychology. It is hoped, too, that in this chapter—as in all future chapters—the door has been opened for the reader to search more deeply into the field.

REVIEW

1. Define personality.
2. What are the two factors upon which personality depends?
3. What factor determines how close a person will come to reaching his potential?
4. Define psychology.
5. How is behavior defined by the psychologist?
6. Note the three false beliefs, disproved by psychologists, which are presented in this chapter.
7. What is the difference between a psychologist and a psychiatrist?
8. What is a psychoanalyst?
9. List and describe the ten fields of psychology.

chapter two

Techniques of Psychological Investigation

"Is he dead?"

"Yeah, I'm afraid so. That brings the total of patrolmen dead up to twelve already this year."

"What about the fellow who shot him? Did they pick him up?"

"Right, homicide division picked him up yesterday. I got a glimpse of him. They've got the goods on him, but he sure doesn't look like the type to be a killer. That's probably how he caught Bob off guard."

"What do you mean?"

"Like I said, he just doesn't look like the type of guy you'd figure to be a killer."

Despite the cliché's warning that "you can't tell a book by its cover," one often makes judgments about people on the basis of a glance. If a man is fat, he must also be jolly; and if he's thin and wears glasses, he must be intelligent. How ridiculous! When people try to make evaluations of human beings solely on the basis of physique or some particular physical characteristics, they are limiting their powers of observation because they are making a decision without all the facts. In the field of law enforcement, as the illustration above demonstrated, this can be fatal. Television producers can decide how a criminal should be dressed. Children can picture what heroes and heroines look like in accordance with the descriptions in their story-books. A man is allowed to decide whether he likes a person living across the street on the basis of the way he walks. However, an evaluation of someone's personality or intelligence on the basis of his physical characteristics is a luxury law enforcement officers cannot afford. Except in the case of a rare disease which alters the victim's appearance—such as microcephaly (abnormally small head), which indicates mental retardation in the individual—the superficial judg-ments one tends to make about people can result in errors that professional law enforcement officers must avoid.

Psychologists make a special effort to avoid making an assumption based only on the facts that are readily available, rather than on all the facts. The use of control is one of the techniques they employ to ensure that they are not trapped into making a hasty judgment.

PSYCHOLOGICAL INVESTIGATION AND CONTROL

Psychology, as a science, uses methods in accordance with the proce-dures employed by other sciences. Thus *control*, which could be considered the essential element in scientific investigations, is applied in psychological studies. Control is present when all the factors in an experiment are held constant and only one variable is allowed to produce the experimental effect. Without it, erroneous conclusions become easy pitfalls for the investigator, as can be seen in the follow-ing simplified example.

Dr. X was commissioned by a company making leather furniture to compare the durability of furniture in which leather was used as a covering and that of furniture where a cotton material was em-ployed. For this small test Dr. X chose eight families—four who had cotton-covered furniture and four who had leather-covered pieces. His results showed that all four families who had the leather furni-ture did in fact have better-looking pieces after two years than those with the cotton-covered furniture. Can his results be questioned? Can the implied generalization that leather wears better than cotton cloth be accepted on the basis of this (imaginary) study? Obviously, the first answer is "yes," the second, "no."

The fact that he didn't control extraneous variables is quite ob-vious. For example, the families with the cotton-covered furniture might have been larger, with many young children. They might have subjected their furniture to more constant rough wear, and this might have been the reason for the difference in the condition of the furniture at the end of two years.

The style of the furniture might have been another factor. Some furniture, by virtue of its design, wears better than other types.

In other words, the conclusion that leather wears better than cotton cannot be drawn from Dr. X's study because he did not control all possible extraneous variables. This point is especially important for the law enforcement and correction officer when he is involved in a criminal investigation or examining any basic on-the-job problem.

Furthermore, even when one tries to be objective and to control for, or at least be open to, possible extraneous variables, personal bias almost always enters into the study. No matter how hard one tries to eliminate his biases, they still enter into the examination process to some extent.[1]

The officer must therefore realize that controlling to eliminate other possible contributing factors is necessary before a final decision is made and, further, that bias is an ever-present, almost unavoidable problem in any investigation since it usually taints the results.

FOUR METHODS OF INVESTIGATION USED IN PSYCHOLOGY

Psychology uses four main techniques of investigation, classified as *experimental, clinical, naturalistic observation*, and *statistical*. Experimental findings are usually widely accepted due to the strict control used in the laboratory to remove extraneous variables. These extraneous variables are elements which should be eliminated so that they won't affect the results of the experiment. Furthermore, experimental research accounts for much of the basic data required by the young science of psychology. Whenever possible, an experiment is the most desirable method of investigation.

However, laboratory conditions are not always practical. When this is the case, it is time for clinical methods and naturalistic observation to come into play. For instance, if a clinical study is to be done on the information gained in an interview of a mentally ill patient by a psychologist, laboratory conditions cannot be imposed. The results obtained will of course be open to a number of interpretations, because the case was unique and the findings could have been influenced by any number of variables, such as the attitude of the therapist toward the patient. Yet, despite the pitfalls, this method does offer information which can be examined and tested

[1] Gunnar Myrdal, *Objectivity in Social Research*, Pantheon, New York, 1969, p. 43.

further; it also demonstrates areas in interviewing and case study techniques which need improvement.

Naturalistic observation is akin to clinical studies, for it too usually lacks strict control. Despite the deficiencies in methodology similar to those listed above, this is another technique which is necessary if the science of psychology is to progress. Mob hysteria is an example of a situation which cannot be controlled by the psychologist. However, it is necessary for him to observe mob hysteria in order to arrive at some facts or hypotheses that can be further examined in an attempt to discover causal relationships. One can then answer questions like "What causes mob actions and reactions?" as well as "Are there similarities between mobs?"

Another type of investigation procedure is based on the science of *statistics*, which aids in classifying the facts the psychologist has gathered. Statistics is *one of the most important tools used in psychological research*. In this capacity it is not only a technique by itself; it is used in the other methods as well. Statistics is useful for a number of reasons:

1. It aids in simplifying and summarizing experimental findings.
2. It facilitates the ability to see trends.
3. It fosters accuracy.

Statistics is an essential subject for all students of psychology. A knowledge of this area is mandatory not only so that one will know how to use statistics, but also so that one can recognize their misuse. For example, many people say that marijuana is dangerous because all the heroin users they know have first used marijuana. They tell marijuana users that they are therefore taking a big chance by smoking it. However, the marijuana user could reply by saying that eating bread must also lead to heroin addiction, because all heroin addicts have eaten sandwiches at some time in their lives prior to becoming addicts. It is hoped that the reader can see the point this example tries to make. Marijuana use *may* indeed lead to heroin use, but the kind of argument cited above could never prove a necessary connection between one situation and the other through the use of statistics. Statistics are very useful, but they can be extremely misleading to those who are not familiar with statistical principles. This fact cannot be overemphasized.

MEASURING PEOPLE

Every individual is unique. Yet people have many common behaviors and responses, and it is possible to group them accordingly. Classification and organization of sections of today's population are proceeding at a fantastic pace in an effort to provide standardized information required by psychologists, sociologists, teachers, corporations, politicians, governments, and others in order to make vital decisions. Colleges are relying on tests to find out whether prospective students possess the required aptitudes to perform well; police departments and religious organizations are administering personality inventories to ensure that they do not mistakenly accept mentally unstable candidates, and military organizations are using tests to identify those individuals who are not trainable or educable. In essence, as noted in a recent article, "Intelligence tests, and the related aptitude tests, have more and more become society's instrument for the selection of human resources."[2]

However, the actual task of measuring people, which is the job psychologists have inherited, is not at all easy to accomplish. Many problems arise when an attempt is made to rate individuals. Psychological testers are often under fire due to the historical belief that measuring any area of man's mental facility is an impossibly presumptuous invasion of human dignity. This feeling, though present to some degree today, is at least no longer as prevalent as it was in the recent past.

Idiographic and Nomothetic Methods

In this vein, Gordon Allport in the 1930s discussed the difference between *nomothetic* and *idiographic* methods of measuring individuals.[3] A nomothetic approach to the rating of human beings is based on a claim that it is possible to describe certain characteristics for all individuals and rate them on a single scale. On the other hand, an idiographic approach is contained in the belief that one should measure only the characteristics unique to each person in order to evaluate him, because men are too humanly particular to be clumped together. Psychology now leans toward the nomothetic approach, using the quantitative rather than the qualitative form of testing. It is not that psychologists don't believe in the individuality of man; the facility and accuracy of the quantitative approach simply makes its use more desirable. However, the idiographic method is still being employed to a certain degree, and examples of both types of techniques will be presented in this chapter.

[2] Richard Herrnstein, "I.Q.," *Atlantic*, September 1971, p. 44.

[3] Gordon W. Allport, *Personality: A Psychological Interpretation*, Holt, Rinehart, New York, 1937.

Intelligence Tests

Psychological tests, if they are sound, should give a true indication of an individual's personality, vocational potential, or intelligence. This section covers some popular tests (those which are widely used as well as those which have proved to be especially accurate) so that the reader may get an indication of the types often used by the correctional psychologist, parole officer, probation officer, court psychologist, correctional counselor, or police applicant screening board, for example. An examination of intelligence tests will be presented first.

The most widely known of this group is the *Stanford-Binet Intelligence Scale.* It can be used accurately with those in the age range of approximately two to thirty-five years. It provides us with the individual's mental age (MA) and his intelligence quotient (IQ).

The term mental age refers to what the average person of a particular age should be expected to accomplish under normal circumstances. The IQ, intelligence quotient, is not the same as mental age. An IQ is designed to tell us how bright a person is compared with other individuals of his own age. According to the prominent psychometric specialist Wechsler, it is "a measure which presumably defines the relative brightness or intellectual possibilities of an individual, *more or less permanently.*"[4] [Italics supplied.] Another test of intelligence is the *Draw a Man* test. In this test the subject is asked to draw a person, and then his drawing is compared to a scale developed by Goodenough. The more complete the drawing, the more intelligent the person is supposed to be.

A third test of intelligence, meant only for adults, is the WAIS (Wechsler Adult Intelligence Scale). It is specified for individuals in their late teens and those up to 60 years old.

A final test in this category is the *Bender Gestalt Test* (also known as the *Visual-Motor Gestalt Test*). It differs from the previous three intelligence-measuring devices in that it is used specifically to uncover intellectual deficiencies. Basically what is required of the person being tested is that he copy nine designs. Ideally, if perceptual distortion is reflected in the reproduction of the designs, this would accurately indicate a mental deficit.

---

[4] David Wechsler, *The Measurement and Appraisal of Adult Intelligence,* Williams and Wilkins, Baltimore, 1958, p. 29.

Vocational Tests

To measure vocational interests there are a number of tests on the market; two of the most widely used are the *Kuder Preference Record—Vocational* and the *Strong Vocational Interest Blank for Men.* These could be used by a counselor, parole officer, or probation officer in employment counseling. However, the accuracy of these types of tests is questionable, so it is necessary to do extensive research into psychological literature on them before deciding to use any particular one on a wide scale.

Objective Personality Tests

Probably the most widely used of its type in existence, the *MMPI* (*Minnesota Multiphasic Personality Inventory*) is a test consisting of 550 elements on which the individual being tested is asked to comment. In each case he describes the relation of the statement to himself by responding "True," "False," or "Cannot say." Within the test there are fourteen scales, four of which are involved in *validity* (checks to see whether the person being tested tried to fake or lie on the test). The interpretation of this test is reflected in the patterns of the scores rather than in the individual answers.

Projective Tests of Personality

Subjective personality tests, referred to as projective tests, are more in keeping with the idiographic approach, which is concerned with the differences within a single individual. The three to be dealt with are: the *Rorschach* (*Ink Blot*) *Test, Make a Picture Story* (*MAPS*), and the *Thematic Apperception Test (TAT).*

In the Rorschach Test the person being tested is asked to comment on a number of standard ink blots. His responses are then scored by the tester as to the attention he gives to color, shape, etc., and finally they are interpreted according to a particular theoretical psychological system.

In the Thematic Apperception Test, rather than ink blots the testee is given a number of pictures and asked to tell a story about the pictures he sees. In the MAPS test, on the other hand, the individual is asked to put cardboard figures on a background which is provided and subsequently to make up a story about them.

The accuracy of the interpretation of these tests is based primarily on the theory of personality used as well as on the experience of the tester. Therefore, the test is somewhat subjective. As a matter of fact, some of these tests require so much subjective interpretation that their value is being questioned by many psychologists.

RELIABILITY AND VALIDITY

In all these tests there is concern about *reliability* (the degree of consistency in the measurement of anything) and *validity*. For a test to be reliable, it should be a standard measuring device for all those tested with it. If it is accurate for one person and inaccurate for others, it is not reliable. For validity to be high in a test, it must measure what it is expected to measure. In other words, if prospective secretaries are given a test to measure efficiency, the test must in fact actually measure efficiency. If applicants score high on the test and then fail on the job in the office, the test is not valid. Therefore, if reliability and validity are not both present to an acceptable degree, the test—no matter how extensive or intricate—is meaningless, and possibly even detrimental if we naively try to predict with it. This is why projective tests, though popular, are often not reliable. In this type of test the interpretation of what is stated by the individual being tested can vary according to what the tester's opinion is. Think of the criminal who is judged by one psychologist or psychiatrist to be mentally incompetent, while another says on the basis of the same projective test that he is normal. This is why an objective inventory such as the MMPI is more widely accepted and used today by psychologists, who tend to be more and more scientific and thus objective in their outlook.

EVALUATION OF POLICE AND CORRECTION OFFICER CANDIDATES

In the process of screening law enforcement and corrections department candidates, some of the tests previously noted could be utilized. However, because of the wide variety of tests and questionnaires currently available, many others are being used in addition to the few listed here.

Though the individual tests themselves may be different, the *types* of tests given (intelligence, personality, and aptitude) remain constant. Usually an intelligence test is given first to screen out those individuals who don't have the ability to learn the duties of the position. If the candidate scores high enough to be considered for admission to the training cycle, he is usually given a personality test and interviewed by a psychologist or psychiatrist. This is to screen out any person who might have a major personality problem.

Once a person is admitted to the force or department, the testing does not end. If he is to be promoted, he must take aptitude tests to determine whether he has the prerequisite knowledge to perform the duties of a sergeant, lieutenant, etc. Unlike the intelligence test, which is designed to see whether he has the ability to learn, the aptitude test is designed to discover what he has learned while on the job.

In the future, if staffing levels in the testing department permit, in addition to the admission tests and interview, follow-up personality tests will also be given to police officers, correction officers, and other front-line law enforcement personnel. The purpose of this re-testing would be to check the personality status of the officer after he has completed several years out in the street or on the prison tiers. If testing reveals that the officer has hardened or become unduly prejudiced, he could be reassigned to an office position on a tempo-rary or permanent basis. Another alternative would be to change his type of job in the field. This change might even alter the situation enough to foster new flexibility in him.

WHAT WAS COVERED IN THIS CHAPTER

This chapter was designed to give an overview of psychological methodology and test types. Intelligence and personality tests were discussed. It was noted that intelligence tests seek to find out how a person is able to perform in relation to his peers, whereas a personal-ity test—be it objective or projective—is designed to determine whether a person has any mental problems.

Psychology uses four main techniques of investigation: experi-mental, clinical, naturalistic observation, and statistical. Special emphasis was placed on statistics, one of the most important tools used in psychological research. Statistics aids in simplifying and sum-marizing experimental findings, facilitating the ability to see trends and fostering accuracy.

Control was also discussed in view of its primary role in scientific investigations. An elementary example was given to show how erro-neous conclusions could be reached if extraneous variables were not controlled in the study of a problem.

In this chapter it was also pointed out that psychology now leans toward the nomothetic approach of discovering individual differ-ences since this quantitative approach is quite accurate and easy to employ.

The final topic covered was the evaluation and reevaluation of police and correction officer candidates. It was brought out that not only is psychological testing important for screening and for use in determining who should be promoted, it can also play a part in reevaluating the outlook of officers who have been on the job for several years to see whether a change has taken place.

REVIEW

1. What is the most important element in scientific investigation?
2. What are the four main techniques of investigation used in psychology?
3. What is one of the most important tools used in psychological research, according to this chapter?
4. What is the difference between the idiographic and nomothetic methods of rating individuals?
5. What are three uses for statistics?
6. In addition to intelligence tests, what other *types* of tests were discussed in this chapter?
7. Define reliability and validity.
8. What would be the purpose of retesting correction and law enforcement officers after they have been in the field for several years?
9. What is an IQ?
10. What kinds of tests are used to screen law enforcement candidates? What is the purpose of giving these tests?
11. What kind of test is given to see whether an officer should be promoted? What is the purpose of this type of test?

chapter three

Learning

Learning is considered by some psychologists to be the most important topic in psychology. Others would agree that it must be ranked at least as one of the most vital areas of study for those seriously interested in the field. Learning is involved in everything one feels and does. It even affects personality. (One's view of oneself and the world is learned.) In addition, as the reader will see after some basic principles have been covered, learning is continually used in law enforcement work, even though its prominence is not often recognized.

DEFINITION OF LEARNING

In a relatively new science such as psychology, special care is taken to define all the terms it uses. This is especially so in the case of a central topic such as learning. For purposes of clarity and simplicity, the following definition will be used: *Learning is a process in which change in behavior occurs.* This definition should be kept in mind, since one of the main points this chapter emphasizes about learning is implicitly contained in it. It is evident that the definition specifically refers to learning as being involved in a process of change in behavior. It does *not* say anything concerning *improvement* in one's behavior as being a necessary part of learning. This is important. Many people unknowingly think of learning as a naturally good thing. This is not so. Often learning results in the acquisition of bad

23

habits and erroneous beliefs. Prejudices as well as skills are learned. To reiterate, then, learning does not always result in improvement! With this in mind, the reader can turn to one of the most significant areas related to the subject of learning—namely, *conditioning*.

CLASSICAL CONDITIONING

Classical conditioning is a basic form of learning which is evident in daily living. A famous experiment that illustrates this type of learning was done by the Russian physiologist Pavlov.[1] In his experiment he used a dog as a subject. In the first step of his procedure he had the salivary duct of the animal channeled outside the cheek so he could easily observe when the dog salivated. Then he noted that the dog salivated upon presentation of a piece of meat. Having recorded this, he presented a light to the dog. The dog did not salivate. The light was noted as being neutral, for it did not elicit the same response that the meat did. Pavlov then proceeded to show the light to the animal just prior to presenting the meat. In other words, he paired the two. The result of the repeated pairings was that he could present the light alone and the animal would salivate. The light, which was previously a neutral stimulus, had taken on the properties of another stimulus—the meat.

In breaking down this well-known illustration of classical conditioning one can arrive at a basic knowledge of a number of technical terms. The four terms used in this illustration are:

1. Unconditioned stimulus (UCS)
2. Unconditioned response (UCR)
3. Conditioned stimulus (CS)
4. Conditioned response (CR)

The unconditioned stimulus, or UCS, is a stimulus which elicits a particular response. This response regularly elicited by a UCS is called an unconditioned response, or UCR. In Pavlov's experiment, the meat that he presented to the dog was the UCS because it regularly elicited a certain response. This response, i.e., salivation, was then the UCR, since it was the usual reaction to the stimulus.

The conditioned stimulus (or CS) is a neutral stimulus. It is neutral because it does *not* elicit the same response as the UCS at the onset of the experiment. In Pavlov's experiment the light used was a condi-

[1] I. P. Pavlov, *Conditioned Reflexes: An Investigation of the Physiological Activity of the Cerebral Cortex*, Oxford University Press, London, 1927.

tioned stimulus. When it was presented to the dog, the dog did not salivate. Therefore, the light qualified as a CS in this experiment.

The next step in the experiment was to pair the light with the meat. First Pavlov showed the light to the dog, then gave him a piece of meat. This process was done a number of times until the light was no longer a neutral stimulus. The dog began to associate the light with the meat, so that Pavlov could present the light by itself and the dog would salivate. This new response to the CS (the light) is called a conditioned response, or CR.

Possibly what Pavlov did can best be understood by breaking it down as follows:

1. UCS (meat) elicits the UCR (salivation).
2. CS (light) is neutral and does not elicit the UCR (salivation).
3. CS (light) is repeatedly paired with the UCS (meat).
4. CS (light) is presented by itself and elicits a new response (salivation), which is called the CR.

Being now somewhat familiar with this basic form of learning, the reader can move out of the laboratory and on to the street to view illustrations of classical conditioning more commonly applied to law enforcement. (Although the illustrations which follow are based on the assumption that behavior which is rewarded is likely to occur more often than unreinforced actions—i.e., that human behavior can be modified—it must be noted that not every psychologist would agree with the conclusions drawn or the learning methods employed. As a matter of fact, those who are neither behaviorists nor eclectics to the point of accepting the principles of reinforcement might even be adamantly opposed to behaviorism: "Human beings are not cattle or dogs and shouldn't be treated as such—animals may be molded by a piece of sugar or a block of salt, but not man!")

The community relations programs of police departments are based—intentionally or unintentionally—on the principle of classical conditioning. If a program can establish an association or pairing between the police (CS) and baseball (UCS), for example, the teen-agers of the neighborhood may transpose their positive feelings toward baseball onto the police force as well. This is part of the success of an organization like PAL (Police Athletic League), for not only does it seek to offer a healthy atmosphere for boys to exercise in, but in the process it also helps the image of the police officer. Here is a breakdown of a police-community relations campaign using the terminology presented above.

1. UCS (baseball) elicits the UCR (pleasure, fun).
2. CS (police) does not elicit a positive response, as baseball does.

3. CS (policeman) is repeatedly paired with the UCS (baseball), because a police officer is the coach of the baseball team.
4. CS (police) elicits a new positive CR.

This example of classical conditioning can easily be compared with Pavlov's experiment. Both illustrations should assist the reader in understanding the concept of classical conditioning. Additional examples of the same principle follow.

In a military correctional facility in Okinawa, those staff members who were involved in treatment wore a uniform different from that of the personnel involved in a security function. Viewed in a somewhat oversimplified manner, the treatment staff (UCS), since their job was to help the confinees, were responded to with trust (UCR). Furthermore, since the treatment personnel wore specific uniforms, the uniform became a symbol of the treatment staff. As a result, someone wearing the uniform (CS) would be responded to with acceptance (CR). With this in mind an experiment was performed. Supervisors were assigned to stay in the dorms wearing the same uniform as that worn by the treatment staff. In this position, the dorm supervisor was able to fulfill an important security function, even though he was technically a member of the treatment staff. The result was that the "jobbings" (muggings) were held to a minimum, since he was in the dorm during the waking hours of the day. In addition, prisoners would often inform him where contraband was being hidden. A breakdown of the experiment is as follows:

1. UCS (treatment staff) elicits a UCR (trust).
2. UCS (treatment staff) wore a particular uniform (CS).
3. CS (uniform) became a symbol of trust because it was worn only by the treatment staff.
4. Dorm supervisors wearing the same uniform as the treatment staff (CS) were responded to in a positive fashion (CR) even though they were performing a semisecurity function.

Another illustration of classical conditioning is the use of the drug Antabuse in treating alcoholics. The following breakdown will show how it works and demonstrate its connection with the principle of classical conditioning.

1. Alcohol (UCS) gives pleasure of some sort (UCR) to the alcoholic.
2. The alcoholic takes Antabuse, which induces vomiting if he drinks an alcoholic beverage.

3. The alcoholic drinks an alcoholic beverage and vomits because of the Antabuse. This process is repeated a number of times.
4. Alcohol (CS) is now avoided (CR) because it induces vomiting instead of pleasure, the earlier UCR.

Now that the reader has seen a few examples of classical conditioning, he should take some time out to reflect upon other possible examples and applications of this principle for the field of law enforcement today.

INSTRUMENTAL CONDITIONING

The other type of conditioning presented in this chapter because of its relationship to learning is instrumental conditioning. This process can be illustrated simply in the following manner. An animal is rewarded if and when he lies down when cued by the words "Get down." By rewarding him *only when he makes the appropriate response*, the trainer is demonstrating a use of instrumental conditioning. Here the animal is instrumental in gaining his own reward. As the reader recalls, in the classical conditioning experiment the unconditioned stimulus—the meat in Pavlov's experiment—was given regardless of what the dog's response was.

A comparison of the two would be profitable because it is easy to confuse classical conditioning with instrumental conditioning. Using the example of disciplinary segregation in a prison as a method of punishment for breaking one of the rules of the institution, let's look first at classical conditioning. John Doe breaks a rule and is sentenced to five days on diminished rations in disciplinary segregation. By this means the security officer is seeking to pair the results of breaking a rule with an unpleasant situation, so that the prisoner is conditioned not to do it again. The five days in solitary is the punishment, which is meant to convince him.

On the other hand, in instrumental conditioning, if he broke the rule he would be sentenced to solitary for an indefinite period. His subsequent release from solitary would depend on his changing his "fight the system" attitude, and his *reward* (release from solitary) *would be contingent* (dependent) *on his actions*. Therefore, the prisoner himself would be instrumental in his own release or reward.

Which type of conditioning is preferable? It's hard to say. It really depends on the situation. In the above comparison the favorable choice seems to be the use of instrumental conditioning, because many prisoners could stand any punishment if they knew how long it would last. In addition, a prisoner usually feels that he deserves to get out of segregation when his set time is up. He may even be released believing that, having paid for his actions, he is free to do as he wants in the future. His delinquency will recur as long as he is willing to pay some price for his behavior.

Giving someone an indefinite time in segregation until he changes his attitude is putting the onus on him. He will be rewarded (get out of "seg") if he wants to be. It's up to him. Another instrumental conditioning technique that could be utilized when someone breaks the rules is to give him a stiff sentence and suspend it. Once again the security staff is leaving it up to him. If he breaks the law while on suspension, he is putting himself in segregation. In instrumental conditioning, then, the individual is trained through the use of reward and punishment to accomplish a specific task or avoid a particular situation.

In fact, the system of parole is also based on the concept of instrumental conditioning. If the prisoner acts in accordance with the rules of the penal community, he is ultimately rewarded with early release. While on parole, if he does not act in line with the terms of his parole and the laws of society, he is punished by being returned to prison.

The use of positive reinforcement (rewards) is also present in the handling of delinquents. Today, many courts and social agencies are setting up *token economies* for adolescent lawbreakers. Under this system a contract is set up between the agency or parents and the youth. If the young person does certain things which are specified in the contract (attends classes, shows respect to parents, etc.), he gets a specified number of tokens. In turn he may exchange these tokens for things which he wants (bicycle, use of the car, etc.). Getting the things the youth wants is then contingent upon whether he behaves in accordance with the contract. This method has proved particularly effective.

In the token economy and in other corrections systems in which rewards and punishments are employed, it is important to realize that the offender is not being "coddled" or appeased. What is happening is that he is being given an incentive—something which he can work for. It is hoped not only that he will seek the rewards by improving his behavior, but also that he will establish a pattern of living which is socially acceptable.

It should also be noted that with psychopaths punishment is almost ineffective, whereas the use of rewards has had significantly positive results. And so, the use of rewards in dealing with criminals appears to have great potential in changing their behavior.

WHAT WAS COVERED IN THIS CHAPTER

Learning, defined as a process in which change in behavior occurs, can play an important role in law enforcement and corrections activities. Illustrations of both classical and instrumental conditioning were given to explain this. Instrumental conditioning was described as being different from classical in that in instrumental conditioning the reward is contingent upon the response of the person. If the individual does not produce the desired response, he is not rewarded.

At this time it appears that learning, a central topic in psychology, will have much to offer the law enforcement and corrections fields as well. Moreover, the good results that have been achieved so far appear to be only the beginning of even more dramatically successful advances.

REVIEW

1. Define learning.
2. Describe Pavlov's experiment.
3. What is the difference between classical and instrumental conditioning?
4. Give two illustrations of how the principles of classical and instrumental conditioning can be applied to the law enforcement or corrections fields.
5. What is the token economy?

chapter four

Emotional Conditions of Man: Frustration, Conflict, and Anxiety

Frustration! Conflict! Anxiety! Everyone today is afflicted to some degree with these emotional conditions. The symptoms they produce range from what we term a "mild upset" to the violent aggression which leads to the murder of one human being by another. However, even though the reader may know about frustration, conflict, and anxiety through experience, much more can be learned about them by briefly examining some of the information which psychologists have gathered. As trained observers of human behavior they have devoted a great deal of time to these three problems. Since law enforcement officers, in particular, deal with individuals who are acting under the influence of one or all of these behavioral conditions, this chapter indeed warrants close attention.

FRUSTRATION

Frustration is the result of something blocking the attainment of a particular goal. Because of this, frustration places stress on the individual and causes him to be tense. In other words, frustration is a form of stress which results in tension.

Frustration, as a type of stress, can be encountered in many forms. It can be a result of internal or external factors; it can be very severe or harmless and almost unnoticeable. Frustration comes in all degrees, in all intensities, and from all directions. Take, for instance,

31

the fisherman's inability to cast far enough to put his lure where he thinks the fish are, or the soldier's discovery in a war zone that his escape route has been blocked by the blowing up of a bridge; both are sources of frustration, though they differ in their impact on the victim's life. The inability to make friends because of a supposed personality flaw is an internal form of stress; prejudice is an external form of stress. Both are examples of frustration.

Just as the strength and type of frustration that affects men is varied, tolerance of frustration also differs. What is terribly frustrating to one person is hardly a bother to another. Furthermore, some things cause people to be tense on some occasions yet fail to arouse them on other occasions. This variance in response to stress has been seriously studied by psychologists. They have been particularly interested in the concept of *frustration tolerance* (the amount of stress—frustration—an individual can take without resorting to the use of an exaggerated form of behavior).

Tolerance of frustration can also be affected by conditions such as *debility* and *dependence.* Comments by former POWs in Korea and Vietnam bear out the fact that these conditions can affect the individual's capacity to deal with frustrations effectively. Debility and dependence in the POW camps were produced in the men by extremely demanding work, little sleep, and lack of sufficient food.

Think how much easier it is for a man to become angered at the end of the workday than it is in mid-morning. Monitoring demonstrations for extended periods of time without being relieved for a lunch and rest break is another example of how physical conditions could adversely affect the frustration tolerance level. Think how much less hostile the officers on crowd control duty would be toward the demonstrators if their superior were able to make arrangements for a temporary relief. And how about the demonstrators who have marched and chanted continuously without eating or relaxing? A long, hard day without letup undoubtedly increases their tendency toward hostility. Therefore, a law enforcement officer should be aware that an incident is more likely to occur as a result of continued frustrations in the instances noted above. In addition, those in a supervisory capacity must realize the human needs of their men and try to arrange a relief system when possible so that frustrations, which can be increased by a lack of food and rest, are kept to a minimum.

This brief view of hostile aggression as a response to frustration brings us to the last element to be covered on this subject—namely, alternate reactions to frustration. It has already been noted that aggression is one type of reaction. There are three others: withdrawal, regression, and inflexibility (fixation).

An example of *withdrawal* can be seen in the apathy that many reformers finally experience after repeated failure to bring about change. Accordingly, in military and government agencies many of the top men who were famous in their youth as tough men of ideals are now considered "wishy-washy," even to the point of laughing at and in some cases resisting the innovations presented by a newcomer who is trying to bring about improvement. Unfortunately, prisons and police departments, too, are often prime examples of this type of resistance to change. Most penal systems are antiquated, and many so-called progressive police departments are in fact resistant to new ideas, appearing unlikely ever to change.

On the optimistic side, though, in the past few years the apathy has faded quite impressively. The fact that law enforcement officers are reading this type of book may be proof of it! In penology alone, more development has taken place in the last three years than in the preceding twenty years.

In addition to aggression and withdrawal, another response to frustration is *inflexibility*. The neurotic who uses exaggerated defense mechanisms which he knows are ineffective typifies this response. How many men find the going tough when they return to school after being away for a long time? And as a result of their inability to cope with the academic experience, they may say that education is useless and that what really matters is "the school of hard knocks" (experience). Everyone knows that there's no substitute for experience. However, education aids an individual to profit from what has happened to him in the past. People who verbally ridicule formal education know this fact, too, though they won't admit it. They are taking an inflexible stance because of the difficulties they would be up against in the classroom, which could result in frustration and loss of face.

A fourth reaction to frustration is *regression*. Learning cursive handwriting is often a frustrating task for children. If they are really having difficulties, they will often revert to printing, and it will take some encouragement on the part of the teacher or parent before the child becomes willing to make another effort and risk failure again. This same principle applies to innovations in a penal system. Naturally, when techniques of behavior modification are newly introduced into a prison, there will be some snags. Yet, despite the fact that, as most people realize, new approaches will require time and effort before they work successfully, those in control may find the new methods frustrating to use and regress to the old ways, which are not working well but with which they are familiar. It is a common form of regression.

At this point, then, having looked at four types of reactions to frustration, a definition of frustration, and the types of frustration, the reader can turn to the topic of *conflict*.

CONFLICT

Conflict is a particular form of internal stress and can actually be considered a type of frustration. There are four ways in which conflict can manifest itself:

1. Approach-approach
2. Approach-avoidance
3. Avoidance-avoidance
4. Double approach-avoidance

Approach-approach conflicts result when an individual is confronted with two desirable goals. (Which of two books should I read?) Approach-avoidance, on the other hand, occurs when an object is both attractive and repulsive. (Going to school is good in that it offers an opportunity to learn, but at the same time sitting in class all day is a confining experience.) Avoidance-avoidance conflict comes about when a choice must be made between two undesirable situations. (This type of conflict is the one often referred to as a dilemma—a "damned if you do, damned if you don't" situation.) Double approach-avoidance is more complex than the previous three discussed. It occurs when one tries to make a decision involving alternatives which both attract and repel at the same time. (A choice between two jobs would be a good example, because both would probably have good points and bad points.)

All four types of conflict cause stress. This stress brings about reactions similar to those of frustration. With this in mind it would be beneficial to discuss another way in which the reaction of aggression can manifest itself when a person is under stress. The method referred to is displacement. *Displacement is the redirection of negative aggression.*

A good illustration of this is as follows. An employee is reprimanded by his boss, and after the individual is "chewed out," he goes home and is grouchy to his wife. What obviously is happening here is that the employee is under stress from his boss, and though he would like to answer him back, he is afraid that if he does he will lose his job. So he displaces (redirects) his anger from his boss to his wife, because she is less threatening to him than his employer.

A similar illustration would be a situation in which an officer assigned to the traffic division is having difficulty advancing in the department, and so (consciously or unconsciously) he decides to vent his pent-up emotions on the motorist with whom he comes in contact.

Prison riots are often the result of displaced aggression. The inmates may be angry because they haven't gone to court yet or because the correction officer does not allow them to have all the freedom they'd like. Since the inmates cannot act out their frustration directly against the court and don't want to be brought up on charges for hitting an officer, they may redirect their aggression. This redirection could take the form of protest over the lack of hot meals. Tables would be turned over—i.e., aggression would be redirected toward these less threatening inanimate objects.

The last aspect to be briefly covered is the part alcohol and drugs play in relation to conflict. Quite simply, it appears that *alcohol and drugs reduce the tendency to avoid a situation.*[1] In the example where the individual was told off by his boss, if he were "under the influence" he might argue with the boss, even though it could cost him his job. Possibly, this further indicates how someone becomes an alcoholic or drug addict. The vicious circle that the individual gets involved in could be as follows: Conflict causes stress, which requires something to reduce the tension (i.e., drugs); the fact that the individual has taken drugs causes him more conflict, so he takes more drugs to relieve the tension, and so on.

At any rate, though conflict is a pertinent area for study by those in law enforcement, the nature of this applied text prohibits exploring it in greater depth. The reader is encouraged to utilize a general psychology text in order to pursue this topic further.

ANXIETY

Anxiety is the result of a vague but often strong concern about an impending danger of some sort. It is not something as well defined as fear. Rather it is an intangible feeling that seems to evade any effort

---

[1] R. A. Clark, "The Projective Measurement of Experimentally Induced Levels of Sexual Motivation," *Journal of Experimental Psychology*, 4, 1952, pp. 391–399.

to resolve it. Its effect on behavior is varied. If it is intense, it can immobilize, whereas if anxiety is low, it can be a motivating force, as in the case of college students. If they are a bit anxious, they tend to study harder.

To reduce the level of anxiety, defense mechanisms are often employed. Since there are so many defense mechanisms, it would be difficult to discuss them all in this chapter. A few will be mentioned so that the reader can have some understanding of what they involve.

Repression is unconscious forgetting. It helps reduce anxiety by removing from the memory any thoughts or impulses which cause anxiety. Another mechanism is *reaction formation.* This technique is used in dealing with unwanted impulses which cause the individual to feel uneasy. A reformed alcoholic who condemns those who drink socially could possibly be using this defense mechanism because he cannot allow himself to think again that drinking might be good under some circumstances. If he does, he might be tempted to start drinking again. Another example of reaction formation, along with other defense mechanisms, will be covered in Chapter 5. For the present, these two defense mechanisms listed should demonstrate what a defense mechanism is and how it is utilized.

Before leaving this area of study on anxiety, the reader should note one final point. Recently studies were done by psychiatrists (Fraser, 1970; Lyons, 1970) on the riots in Belfast, Northern Ireland. One of the observations was that there was an increase in the level of anxiety in sections bordering ghetto-riot areas. Furthermore, it was mentioned that rioting, unlike war, does not result in people pulling together. This study is relevant in the United States because law enforcement officials have to patrol ghettos and deal with the people who live there. It can be inferred that in these ghettos anxiety is high, as it was in Belfast, because there are mothers with large families who, if burned out, have no place to go. In addition, if their neighborhood stores are destroyed, they may not be able to get to the stores that are five miles away because of lack of transportation. Therefore, for law enforcement personnel anxiety is a very pertinent subject that ought to be thoroughly understood.

WHAT WAS COVERED IN THIS CHAPTER

Frustration, the result of something blocking the attainment of a particular goal, is increased when an individual is deprived of rest or is under continual pressure. Conflict, another type of stress mentioned, involves four situations: approach-approach, approach-avoidance, avoidance-avoidance, and double approach-avoidance. Anxiety, the third emotional condition covered, can have various effects depending upon its degree. It was noted that anxiety, when it is low, can act as a motivating force. However, when anxiety is high, it can immobilize the individual or cause him to resort to the use of defense mechanisms in order to cope with the situation.

The large majority of people one meets as a law enforcement officer will probably be under stress from some combination of the emotional conditions dealt with in this chapter. A job is generally easier and more satisfying if one is capable of appreciating the emotional needs of the people with whom he comes in contact. Furthermore, it is hoped that this chapter will help the reader to understand his own feelings and actions as well as those of his supervisors and subordinates.

REVIEW

1. Define frustration.
2. What is frustration tolerance?
3. What are the four types of reactions to frustration?
4. Define conflict.
5. Give four ways in which conflict can manifest itself.
6. Define anxiety.

section two

Abnormal Psychology

chapter five

Neurosis
and Psychosis

Neurosis and *psychosis* are terms used to describe the mental status of certain psychologically unstable individuals. They are frequently used in reports and articles and even in everyday conversation, so today's professional law enforcement personnel are expected to be familiar with them. A knowledge of both psychotic and neurotic symptoms and reactions should prove to be particularly useful to those who must deal with the psychologically ill on the street or in the prison system.

WHO IS A NEUROTIC?

Neurosis is a common psychological disorder, and neurotic symptoms are present to a certain degree in everyone. What differentiates the "normal" individual from the person categorized as a neurotic is the *degree* to which those symptoms are present. Everyone utilizes defense mechanisms such as forgetting. Unconsciously people tend to put bothersome things out of their minds. However, a neurotic is an individual who uses exaggerated defense mechanisms. Instead of just forgetting, the neurotic may actually develop amnesia. So even though everyone uses defense mechanisms to some extent, a person becomes classified as a neurotic when:

1. His use of defense mechanisms interferes with his daily activities.
2. People start to notice that he is acting abnormally.

It is very difficult to distinguish the neurotic from the eccentric, because the line between normal and abnormal is blurred. Laymen and psychologists alike are still questioning how distorted a man's perceptions must be to classify him as a neurotic. The two points previously noted can perhaps serve at least as a guide for the student.

DEFENSE MECHANISMS

Since the utilization of defense mechanisms (unconscious techniques used to prevent a man's self-image from being damaged) is an important factor in any discussion of neurosis, a thorough examination of a number of them is in order at this time. The following will be examined here: denial, rationalization, regression, identification, reaction formation, projection, acting out, compensation, intellectualization, sympathism, fantasy, and compromise formation. Once again it is emphasized that all of us use defense mechanisms; it is the exaggerated use of them that causes a person to be classified as a neurotic.

Denial as a technique involves a method of evasion in which the individual simply avoids something that is unpleasant. Students often refuse to think about the homework that's due the next day and get involved in anything except what they're supposed to be doing—studying their assignments. Another example might be the detective on a case who spends many hours interviewing everyone but the prime suspect, who happens to be from a ghetto area where two police officers were murdered the previous month.

Rationalization is used to justify and excuse an individual's behavior to himself and others. A seemingly hard-working, dedicated employee caught pilfering goods from his employer rationalized his dishonesty by saying that "the boss has so much, he wouldn't miss a lousy shirt." However, when his house was searched, $1,500 worth of stolen goods were uncovered. Faced with this discovery, he further rationalized: "With what he was paying me, he owed me at least that much to make up for my putting out like I did."

Regression is another mechanism. In this technique the individual reverts to a past behavior. This might be typified by the thirty-year-old escaped prisoner who thinks and talks about his parents while on the run. In doing this he is recalling and trying to recapture the secure life he had with his parents at a time when, by contrast, his whole future is highly insecure.

Identification is used so that a person can associate himself with something or someone in order to elevate his position. Those who organize a community relations campaign or an "open house at the station house" are hoping that local youths will be motivated to identify with the police and their work. In Washington, D.C., the FBI has an elaborate demonstration which is provided for the public. It is performed with the belief that visitors will respect the Bureau, want to identify with its agents, and cooperate with them should the need arise.

Reaction formation occurs when someone tries to prevent his submission to unacceptable impulses by vigorously taking an opposite stand. While counseling addicts in New York, the author found an interesting illustration of this around voting time. Many of the addicts, though confessed and convicted criminals, vehemently professed a deep belief and trust in the "law and order" candidate, as if they were trying to demonstrate that they were really on the right side of the law.

Similar to reaction formation is *projection*. It is a method in which we attribute to others our own faults in an effort to prevent ourselves from being blamed. When a handcuffed killer escapes because the officer failed to utilize the proper security precautions, and the officer blames the force because "the force doesn't provide leg irons in their squad cars," projection might be the driving force behind the officer's complaint.

In *acting out*, the individual deals with all his impulses by expressing them. The youth who wrecks a bar when refused a drink because he's under age is probably responding to this mechanism, which is typified by his inappropriate and unrestrained expression of anger.

Compensation is an attempt to deal with one deficiency by concentrating on another area. This can be beneficial, as in the case of a blind person who compensates for his loss by learning to utilize more fully his senses of touch and hearing. However, it also can be harmful, as in the case of an unpopular, short, inferior man who develops his marksmanship ability and becomes the "enforcer" for a protection racket. He is trying to compensate for his inadequacies by wrongfully displaying his power with a gun.

Intellectualization serves to cut off the emotions from a situation which normally is full of feeling. The "enforcer" for an organized crime syndicate who kills for a living and the prostitute who sells herself on the street could both be utilizing this means of defense against their emotions by eliminating feeling from their activities.

Sympathism is a commonly used technique of defense in which a person seeks to be praised or to have his spirits lifted by relating his faults or problems. In an effort to get the store to release him, the shoplifter will often employ this method to arouse sympathy when caught. Another example is the traffic violator who tells the story of his life in an effort to get the officer to feel sorry for him and let him off without a summons.

Fantasy is also classified as a defense mechanism. It is typified by the frequent daydreamer who is paying attention not to what is going on around him, but rather to what is taking place in his thoughts—events which are embellished by his imagination. The delinquent dropout who is not willing to put forth any effort yet believes that he will be a great man someday is another example. Fantasy could be blamed in the case of the correction officer who is on a boring assignment, has not been rotated in months, and is swept up thinking about last year's vacation, his children, his home, etc.; ultimately his daydreaming causes him to miss contraband being brought into the prison through his post because his mind was not on his duties.

Compromise formation is the last mechanism to be explained. The best example of it is the barbed comment. One student who dislikes another might say to him after a class, "Boy, your essay was good . . . did you write it all by yourself?" As you can see, there are two opposite sentiments contained in the statement. Often witnesses who are hostile to the prime suspect will start off by noting that they don't want to get the defendant into any trouble, *but* . . .

A number of defense mechanisms have been illustrated. They are used by everyone, and the reader should try to spot them in himself as well as in others. Defense mechanisms are for the most part inappropriate means used to deal with stress and therefore should be eliminated as much as possible. If a man is unhappy with his life, dreaming about faraway lands is going to make him feel better *temporarily*. However, fantasy of this sort will never offer a permanent answer. Therefore it is suggested that the reader review the defense mechanisms listed above to see how many of them personally apply to some extent. With a knowledge of defense mechanisms and a reflection on personal response to everyday problems, the reader could reap the reward of being able to improve and be more at ease with himself.

In addition, being familiar with this area will enable a law enforcement agent to recognize the ways in which others employ defense mechanisms. This knowledge should aid the officer in weeding through the personality mazes which some individuals set up to prevent the officer from finding the truth in their statements.

NEUROTIC SYMPTOMS

At this level of inquiry, a textbook of an applied nature could not and should not delve deeply into the causes of neurosis. Yet it would be profitable for law enforcement officers to be at least introduced to the symptom patterns. Six primary symptom patterns will be covered here. They are chiefly characterized by the following symptoms:

1. Anxiety
2. Phobia
3. Depression
4. Obsessions
5. Asthenic reaction (neurasthenia)
6. Hysteria

In the type of neurosis characterized by *anxiety* the individual is extremely apprehensive, is quite upset, has continual waves of panic, and is psychologically and physically tense. When questioned he relates the feeling that his occupational position, future, conscience, or even his life is vaguely threatened. This symptom pattern of anxiety, which is the most common of the six, can cause the neurotic to vomit, lose his balance, or even commit suicide.

In dealing with an individual of this nature great care is needed, and an attitude of calm, sincere interest must be employed. A show of nervousness or a lack of genuineness and concern could cause him to become worse. For example, in a city corrections facility on the East Coast a young, extremely anxious inmate threatened to jump off the third tier of one of the cell blocks. The other prisoners jeered him on, while the correction officer yelled, "Don't jump! I'm coming to get you." The youth jumped when the officer started to run up the stairs to reach him. In this instance the correction officer precipitated the unfortunate outcome. The officer should have first attempted to quiet the block. Then he should have attempted to talk the inmate down, while inching up the stairs slowly. Any quick action with an anxious individual can be dangerous.

In a prison, desirable methods of handling such individuals include use of tranquilizers, professional counselling, and confinement in administrative segregation until hospitalization is possible. Officers in the field should realize that alcohol and pills are often used by anxiety-ridden neurotics and can contribute to the complexity of handling them. Medical attention is essential as soon as possible after an individual of this type is apprehended.

Another symptom that can be noticeably present is a *phobia*. A phobia is a constant fear of something that presents no actual threat or that should be, at the very most only bothersome. Some common phobias are:

1. Fear of closed places—claustrophobia
2. Fear of fire—pyrophobia
3. Fear of crowds—ochlophobia
4. Fear of high places—acrophobia

In neurotics the manifestation of one or more of these indicates an attempt to avoid some internal or external danger which *they feel* is present. It is the best way they know to defend themselves.

In neurotics, *depression* can also be present. It is marked by feelings of discouragement, dejection, sadness, and a very negative attitude toward themselves. Furthermore, many neurotics have lost one of the most vital human techniques of adaptation—their sense of humor. Law enforcement officers must always take careful security measures with this type of individual so that suicide is not presented as an easy alternative.

In prison, any medicine provided for a person suffering from extreme depression should be administered by the officer, or its use should be monitored by him because a prisoner with this condition might logically infer that nothing can help, even medical assistance, and might stop taking what was prescribed for him. He might also hoard the pills to commit suicide.

An *obsessive-compulsive* reaction can also be a manifestation of neurosis. This technique is used so that the individual can control his anxiety. As strange as it sounds, the neurotic is aware of the unusual nature of his compulsive acts and obsessional thoughts. Obsessions usually center on a fear that one will submit to an uncontrollable impulse to do something wrong. Compulsive acts such as stepping over cracks in the sidewalk are performed by many people during the day. Yet, characteristically, neurosis involves compulsions which are so much more exaggerated and irrational.

Asthenic reaction (neurasthenia) is still another possible neurotic reaction. This symptom is characterized by fatigue and many other physical complaints. It is considered to be caused by an individual's belief that life is hopeless.

The final neurotic symptom to be treated here is *hysteria*. Hysteria, or conversion reaction, as it is now called, takes in two symptom areas: illness without physical cause and dissociative reactions such as amnesia and somnambulism (sleepwalking). Illness without physical cause could include loss of appetite, loss of sensitivity in certain areas of the body, choking sensations, and an inability to walk or talk. These symptoms are not as evident today as they were in the past. People, and the services available to them, have become sophisticated to the point where this type of reaction is not socially acceptable any more. And though it may be hard to believe, most neurotics use the techniques of defense that seem to be most credible. In addition, since psychological and psychiatric services have become so advanced, the ignorance which prevailed up to World War II in dealing with this symptom has been replaced by some superb diagnostic and therapeutic techniques. Some examples of hysteria in terms of illness without physical cause are:

1. Astasia-abasia—inability to control legs when standing
2. Aphonia—inability to speak
3. Anesthesia—loss of sensitivity
4. Analgesia—loss of pain

Dissociative reactions are also under the symptom category of hysteria. Examples of dissociative reactions are:

1. Amnesia—complete or partial loss of memory
2. Fugue—flight from a life situation
3. Somnambulism—sleepwalking
4. Multiple personalities

The only symptom above that is difficult to recognize is fugue. It is a reaction in which the individual flees without conscious awareness from his home situation for a period of time. And in some rare instances the individual leaves home and the stressful situation in which he is involved to take on a completely new life. Two other points that should be noted are:

1. Neurotics with multiple personalities are rare.
2. Sleepwalkers (somnambulists) can harm themselves during this state and should be awakened to prevent possible injury.

These six primary symptom patterns of neurosis should give the student a clearer understanding of how to recognize this condition and how to handle individuals afflicted by it.

HANDLING MARITAL PROBLEMS

No discussion of neurosis, the most common form of abnormal behavior, would be complete without mentioning the violent neurotic episodes which involve two or more members of the same immediate family.

Perhaps the most difficult police function is intervention in family crisis situations. Studies have estimated that family disturbance calls are one of the leading causes of police fatalities in the line of duty and account for 40 percent of the time lost due to disabilities resulting from injuries. Other studies have shown that such calls for police assistance are common to rural as well as to urban centers. One police official, drawing on extensive rural experience, estimates that "family fights" are second in frequency only to motor vehicle accidents as incidents involving police action.[1]

Dealing with marital disputes can sometimes present great difficulties for the officer who is not trained in dealing with family problems. Here are 16 of the 19 steps designated by Selwyn Lederman, Ph.D., in a report for a government project on family problems, as effective methods of intervening in family disputes which the officer can apply when arriving on the scene.

1. Prevent violence by separating the disputants.
2. Allow only one person to talk at a time.
3. Take the disputants into separate rooms.
4. Switch officers so that the stories can be checked out.
5. In listening to the stories, try to find out in each case what each individual contributed to the conflict.
6. If one of the disputants holds himself to blame, find out in what ways the other shares the blame.
7. Ask questions so as to get the details as clear as possible.
8. Find out if there has been a previous history of this kind of behavior.
9. See if the history goes back to before the marriage, other relationships, or similar relationships in the present.
10. Give each person the opportunity to speak in detail.

[1] Morton Bard, *Training Police as Specialists in Family Crisis Intervention*, U.S. Government Printing Office, Washington, D.C., 1970, p. iii.

11. Bring the couple together to tell their stories to each other. Again, make sure only one person speaks at a time.
12. Point out similarities and discrepancies in the stories.
13. Point out the part that each is playing.
14. Get a reaction from both about what the officers say they see is going on.
15. Ask what the couple plan to do in response to what has transpired and to the officers' reactions. If they seem to understand and say they want to try to work it out, accept it.
16. If you disagree with their response, suggest that they seek other help.[2]

The officer should realize that when he arrives on the scene, he will often be encountering a situation in which he can do great good or great harm, since both parties will be emotionally drained by the argument and the physical presence of the police. While they are in this state, they are amenable to almost anything said by the officer. This is why it is important for the above steps to be understood and followed.

If physical separation is necessary, the officer must also remember that the person holding the lease or mortgage cannot legally be forced to leave the premises. Therefore, in the case of the husband holding the lease, the wife can be advised to move to a friend, relative, etc., for the time being.

WHAT IS PSYCHOSIS?

Psychosis is the denial of major aspects of reality. When an individual is a psychotic, he is partially cut off from his environment. To illustrate this it would be helpful to look at a hypothetical person who becomes psychotic. (For purposes of instruction the example used is oversimplified.)

John D. was raised to be completely immersed in basketball. His father repeatedly taught him to look upon basketball not only as a sport but also as the direct route to fame and fortune. When John got up in the morning, he would immediately turn to the newspaper's sports page. He even had the team standings memorized. In high school, he made the team as a substitute, though it was only through bullying the other players that he managed to get accepted

[2] *Ibid.*, p. 19.

at all. When he played, if he made a mistake, his father would beat him; if he did well, he was treated like a king. Upon entering college he tried out for the team. Competition being much keener at this level, he was informed at the beginning of tryouts that "he couldn't make the team in a million years." Despite this abrupt brush-off by the coach, he returned day after day when practice was scheduled. At first he pleaded with the coach to put him on the team as a substitute, noting that he had great potential. When his request was continually refused, his pleading turned into demanding, and finally one afternoon he was ejected from the court because he was becoming extremely annoying and irrationally emotional—sometimes he would scream that he was a great basketball star and no one was smart enough to realize it. After being banned from the gym, he started to cut classes frequently and was usually found in his room looking at sports magazines, until he finally was brought to the attention of the school authorities. His reaction to this subsequently resulted in his being admitted to a psychiatric hospital, but instead of believing himself to be John D. he now claimed to be a great basketball player on the Boston Celtics. He had cut himself off from reality, so that now he was the greatest basketball player he knew rather than the failure he didn't want to know.

This example should adequately illustrate how a person can become psychotic and should give an indication of what the definition "denial of reality" means. At this point it would be appropriate to look at four psychotic symptom patterns. They are:

1. Schizophrenic reactions
2. Paranoid type reactions
3. Affective reactions
4. Involutional reactions

To avoid confusion it should be realized that just as the line separating the neurotic and the "normal" person is blurred, there is no clear delineation separating neurosis from psychosis. It is again a case of degree. Though neurotics and psychotics often manifest similar symptoms, the neurotic would probably still be able to function in the world, whereas *the psychotic is so divorced from life that he usually must be hospitalized.*

Psychotic individuals are also suicide risks. This is especially so in the case of persons who were previously hospitalized for a serious mental illness. Within one month after release from a mental institution the psychotic may become anxious or depressed in his new environment and attempt suicide because:

1. He is intensely lonely, empty, and he feels terribly cut off from the world.
2. He may be hearing voices which are telling him to kill himself.
3. He may be seeing, hearing, or in some other manner sensing things which are frightening him.

In the above instances, the person can often be helped through the use of antidepressant drugs and psychotherapy. He should be referred for medical or psychological examination when the above symptoms are observed.

SCHIZOPHRENIC REACTIONS

Schizophrenia, the most common psychotic reaction, includes symptoms which affect the emotional and intellectual processes. One symptom of the schizophrenic is a lack of concern with what is going on around him. He seems to be disinterested in everything, extremely withdrawn and autistic. In addition, schizophrenics often manifest little or no emotion and act in an unusual manner, doing things that typify people who are thought of as insane. Schizophrenics also hallucinate and have delusions. All of these symptoms are further classified into types, which will not be included here. It is sufficient if the reader can become familiar with the major symptoms of schizophrenia.

PARANOID TYPE REACTIONS

Paranoia and the paranoid state are both developed symptoms of psychosis. Both symptoms are similar in that they are based on strongly held false beliefs. The difference between the two is that paranoia is more developed and permanent than the paranoid state. The main point to remember about individuals with paranoid type symptoms is that they can sometimes be quite convincing. In addition, they can be dangerous. The paranoid individual often has a delusion which is based on the belief that people are "after him." Therefore, it is common for him to strike out against those whom he thinks are involved in this plot. An illustration of both facts, namely, that a paranoid can be convincing and dangerous, is contained in the following actual case history.

A senior student nurse was assigned to the admissions building of a psychiatric institution after being instructed in the academic theories and problems of psychiatric care. Here she came in contact with a quiet, cooperative male Negro patient. For three weeks she spoke with him daily, and on the basis of these conversations he appeared to be intelligent, well-mannered, and "normal." Among other more general topics, the patient logically explained how his admission to a psychiatric hospital was a case of mistaken identity.

At the end of three weeks the patient had the nurse convinced that a terrible mistake had been made. At the beginning of the fourth week, the nurse was about to discuss the above patient with the house psychiatrist, when the entire picture changed. The patient approached the nurse stating that he had tested her and knew that he could trust her. He then told the story which is outlined below.

First he stated that he was not actually a Negro but that his blond hair, blue eyes, and fair skin had gradually become darker over a period of fifteen years. He went on to talk of the plots against him to prevent him from arriving at various destinations. For example, when he was crossing the Verrazano Bridge, "they" turned it around so that he ended up on the same side from which he had started. "They" constantly rearranged entire neighborhoods so that he was unable to locate the homes of friends and relatives. Lastly, he was being taken advantage of because he was half man and half woman and no one would believe him.

After this sudden revelation by the patient, the nurse was granted permission to review the patient's case history, which included the following points. The patient received a general discharge from military service, was unable to hold down a job for more than a few months at a time, and had a police record for charges of vagrancy and disorderly conduct. Finally, on the night of his admission to the psychiatric institution, he had been arrested for the murder of an innocent man in a local bar. His ravings about plots and invisible enemies after his arrest led to the request for his psychiatric evaluation.

This example indicates how logical a paranoid individual can be at times. Is it any wonder that such a person is so dangerous? Finding out in time that the individual is paranoid could mean the difference between life and death for the individual dealing with him. If the paranoid falsely believes that you are part of a plot to "get him," it would not be surprising if he attempted to "get you first." A psychotic who is paranoid, probably more than any other type of psychologically ill person, should be hospitalized in a mental institution.

AFFECTIVE REACTIONS

In affective reactions the psychotic manifests a seriously unrealistic *mood* disorder. In this disorder the individual can be:

1. Severely depressed
2. Manic-depressive (on top of the world for a time, then subsequently convinced of his utter worthlessness)

Involutional psychotics can also be included in this symptom pattern because they show evidence of depression, which particularly occurs in late middle age.

So, whether the individual is suffering from severe depression or is a manic-depressive, he can be considered as involved in an affective type reaction or as symptomatically revealing a severe mood disorder. As one would expect, a severely depressed psychotic is a security risk since he might be tempted to commit suicide.

SUICIDE IN A CORRECTIONAL FACILITY

Suicide may be attempted by both the neurotic and psychotic individual. However, the normal person may also attempt it if he is put under enough stress. Any one of the following factors or a combination thereof could eventually cause enough pressure to build up in a normal inmate to cause him to commit suicide:

1. Bad news, or no news, from home
2. Continual confinement in a small cell with another person
3. Homosexual rape
4. Receiving a beating from an inmate or correction officer
5. Confinement for a long duration while in an unsentenced status

When he is under stress from something which might result in a suicide attempt, there are usually signs of his depression which the correction officer can observe. For example, depression might be indicated if the inmate seems:

1. Withdrawn
2. Sad
3. Lethargic
4. Unable to sleep, eat, or care for himself
5. Preoccupied with failure, guilt, or death

The person really wanting to kill himself will usually attempt it immediately after the officer finishes his check of the cellblock. The manipulator, on the other hand, will often make an attempt just prior to the beginning of the officer's check. However, despite this rule of thumb, it is almost impossible to discriminate accurately between someone who is trying to kill himself and someone who is making a false attempt as a means of manipulation. Therefore, all suicide attempts should be taken as bona fide.

Suicide attempts may also be made by homosexuals as a flamboyant gesture. Sometimes when a homosexual loses his male lover he may, like a spurned woman, attempt to get him back by trying to kill himself. Since this attempt is not usually genuine, and because homosexuals are involved, the officer may tend to overlook the occurrence. Yet when suicide is attempted, it must always be taken seriously. Numerous deaths have taken place in cases where the person attempting suicide did not really plan to go through with it but accidentally lost his life because of poor judgment on his part.

THE MENTALLY ILL AND THE LAW ENFORCEMENT OFFICER

In addition to the important topics already discussed in this chapter, the following are especially relevant for the law enforcement and correction officer because of their applied nature:

1. Recognizing the gross symptoms of mental illness
2. Handling the mentally ill

No foolproof checklist can be given to the officer to enable him to determine who is mentally ill. Psychiatrists, psychologists, and other professionals in the mental health field study for years and use sophisticated techniques to determine whether someone is actually mentally ill. However, it is possible to list a number of symptoms of *gross* mental illness. A person with an extreme mental disorder may be tentatively distinguished if he manifests all or some of the following behavior(s):

1. Has unusual sense experiences:
    a. Hears voices or noises which no else hears.
    b. Smells peculiar odors of which nobody else is aware.
    c. Sees strange things that aren't present.
    d. Feels pain without an apparent cause for it.

2. Expresses extreme fears or outlandish ideas:
   a. Believes people are watching him or are threatening his life.
   b. Has grandiose ideas about himself—thinks he is somebody who is well known or who has great power.
3. Is manifesting a new, unaccountable type of behavior:
   a. Has changed his pace of living radically—has become extremely active or particularly lethargic.
   b. Has become disinterested in life, is irresponsible, or is quite prone to sudden violence.
4. Has a strange, significant loss of memory.

Most of the above information can be obtained through direct observation and by talking to the individual's family and friends.

Once the officer arrives and evaluates the situation as one in which an apparently mentally disturbed person is involved, he must see that the individual doesn't hurt himself or others. The cardinal rule in handling such persons is: *Don't agitate the individual; do all in your power to provide a nonthreatening environment.* This can be done by taking the following measures:

1. Present a composed appearance when approaching the individual.
2. Don't give the impression that you are in a hurry. (If he appears violent, wait until he calms down before approaching him, unless his life or the lives of others are in *immediate* danger.)
3. Speak with a normal, but firm, voice.
4. Be aware that the disturbed person may attempt to excite and annoy anyone trying to help him. This can be done with insults or comments used in an effort to bait the officer. The mentally disturbed person is not responsible for these remarks, since they are only symptoms of his problem. Understanding that the disturbed person may try to get the officer upset is important, because such an individual may be particularly adept at finding the officer's sensitive point.
5. Don't try to deal with the person yourself. Enlist the aid of those people he is familiar with, such as neighbors or family members.

Usually force will not be required when dealing with a mentally disturbed person. However, the officer should always be alert to the *possible* dangers involved when handling this type of individual, even if he presently appears quite calm. If force is necessary to subdue a disturbed person, there is no reason why he or the officer should become injured. Physical injury seldom results in mental institutions when restraints are applied, because those in charge use the proper methods. The same success can be achieved by the officer if he follows these guidelines when it becomes necessary to subdue a disturbed person:

1. The person should be maneuvered into an area where he is least likely to be hurt upon being restrained.
2. One officer should not attempt to overcome a disturbed person by himself. Often the latter's state provides him with an ability to muster up short bursts of extreme strength.
3. If the use of restraints is necessary, any large cloth object (blanket, tablecloth, sheet) will do. Handcuffs and other metallic devices should not be used, since the person may cut his wrists on them.

If the officer handles the excited, possibly dangerous disturbed individual in a calm, quick manner, utilizing the above points as a guide, the resulting problems (if any) should be minimal. Handling disturbed individuals—even those who do not become unruly—is a difficult job at best. An informed officer who can deal with the situation effectively should be able to avoid the unpleasantness which occurs when an officer abruptly arrives on the scene and resorts to threats and unnecessary force. Knowing what to do in difficult instances will remove much of the insecurity which prompts rash, inappropriate action. Therefore, the importance of understanding what has just been covered cannot be overemphasized.

WHAT WAS COVERED IN THIS CHAPTER

This chapter dealt with the symptoms of neurosis and psychosis and also the psychiatric classifications of psychosis. Early in the chapter it was explained that even the "normal" individual utilizes defense mechanisms to some degree, whereas a neurotic uses defense mechanisms in an *exaggerated* form.

Emphasis was placed on the fact that a neurotic is still able to cope with his environment but the psychotic, with his denial of reality, usually requires hospitalization. The main point of this information for law enforcement officers is simply that a psychotic, regardless of the character of his crime, needs more than just confinement because psychosis is a serious illness.

Such an attitude would serve as a definite asset in the ultimate pursuit of safeguarding society. For what is the purpose of imprisoning and then paroling a psychotic when the basic problem is not his crime but rather his illness or inability to cope with the demands of society? Confinement, in itself, will not cure the psychotic. And his release will only succeed in returning the problem to the streets, where it doesn't belong!

REVIEW

1. What differentiates the "normal" individual from the person categorized as a neurotic?
2. What are defense mechanisms?
3. Describe and give an illustration for each of the following defense mechanisms:

   (a) denial
   (b) rationalization
   (c) regression
   (d) identification
   (e) reaction formation
   (f) projection

   (g) acting out
   (h) compensation
   (i) intellectualization
   (j) sympathism
   (k) fantasy
   (l) compromise formation

4. Neurotic symptoms are chiefly characterized by six symptoms. What are they?
5. What is the most common symptom of neurosis?
6. Define phobia.
7. What is psychosis?
8. Why is a paranoid individual dangerous?
9. What symptoms were presented so that the officer could recognize gross mental illness?
10. What are four measures to be followed in handling a mentally disturbed person?
11. What are three points to remember in subduing a dangerously disturbed person?

chapter six

Sociopathic Personality Disorders

Of all the various psychological disorders which law enforcement and correction officers should become familiar with, probably the most important category is that of the sociopathic personality disorders. A full understanding of this group is desirable. A sociopathic disorder is one form of a *character disorder*. A character disorder results mainly from *faulty development* rather than from stress pressuring the individual's mental makeup. In other words, the individual who is suffering from a character disorder may have been subjected to an unusual family or neighborhood background which advocated certain inappropriate methods of dealing with life, methods which are not in keeping with the rules of society as a whole.

This is essentially true in the case of a sociopath. For example, if his friends indicate that it is all right to steal to get what he wants, the individual may feel that stealing is good and therefore experience no guilt when he commits such an act. As a result, the individual doesn't become concerned about his actions, even when caught. The formerly common slang phrase "Don't sweat it" indeed refers to those suffering from a type of character disorder—especially those characterized as sociopaths, the subjects of this chapter as well as Chapters 7 and 8. This type of individual, who has little or no conscience, does not "sweat" (worry) about his misdeeds, for he has been brought up to view them as acceptable.

The classification "sociopathic personality disorder" is a sub-

category of the group known as character disorders, and it in turn
has subcategories. There are four different types of sociopathic
personality disorders. They are:

1. Antisocial reaction
2. Dyssocial reaction
3. Sexual deviation
4. Addiction

In this chapter the first three reactions will be discussed. Alcohol
and drug addiction will be covered in Chapters 7 and 8, since due to
their importance they require a more thorough treatment.

ANTISOCIAL REACTION (PSYCHOPATHIC REACTION)

First, the antisocial (also called *psychopathic*) reaction will be
discussed. The main characteristic of a psychopath is the almost
complete absence of an ethical or moral fiber. This trait, when
combined with the fact that an antisocial person is usually unable to
follow socially accepted rules and norms of behavior, results in the
individual's having continuous problems with the law.

The fact that the psychopath, for the most part, does not learn
what he should do from what he has experienced in the past
complicates this situation even more. This is especially true in the
instance where he is punished for his antisocial acts, and it has
horrible implications and consequences for society. Most of the
antiquated criminal justice systems in the world are built on the use
of punishment as a deterrent against the commission of future
crimes. Since it doesn't have any effect on the psychopath, nothing is
being accomplished by its use!

To illustrate the typical reaction of an antisocial person, the
following fictional account is given.

John S. was constantly seeking personal pleasure and enjoyment—
fun was his main goal; he seemed to live from moment to moment.
Partly because of this, he was liked by many of his peers.

A high school dropout, he decided it would be fun to visit the
local college toward dusk on a Saturday, one particular week in the
fall of 1969. He entered the student lounge on campus and within
one hour had broken a statue, cut up a painting, and stabbed a
security guard with a small penknife.

Upon apprehension he showed no concern over his misdeeds but only looked puzzled and uttered in a low voice, "I was just having a little fun."

In the light of this example, a closer examination of some of the charcteristics of the antisocial person can now be made. The characteristics covered will be:

1. Absence of guilt and tension
2. Undeveloped conscience
3. Inadequate personal relations
4. Impulsive and irresponsible nature
5. Inability to profit from experience

A psychopath will often deal with his tensions by simply "acting out." Therefore, aggression is a technique generally used by an antisocial individual. If something is upsetting him, he simply strikes out against it. In addition, since guilt is lacking in this type of individual, he often escapes suspicion after he has committed an offense. He can use an outrageous lie so convincingly that he is often believed. He's adept at "conning" people; in prisons many a warden and counselor have been fooled by this type of sociopath.

One factor which accounts for his lack of guilt, referred to above, is his backward conscience. In examining the psychopath's IQ one is able to see that his intellectual development seems to far outdistance the maturity of his conscience. The antisocial person is often quite intelligent but shows little or no evidence of having developed moral fiber.

In referring to a psychopath's ability to interact personally with others, one can hardly avoid the use of negatives. The antisocial individual is *not* grateful, *not* sorry, *not* sympathetic, and *not* dependable. In essence he could not care less about the people with whom he comes into contact.

Furthermore, he is unable to withstand any appreciable degree of frustration. Thus he is often involved in crimes that feature sex gratification and thrills. Somehow he feels that he will evade apprehension and punishment. He considers the pleasure of the moment to be the only thing that is important. He cannot put off for the future anything that appeals to him, and the past has no real meaning for him.

This relates to the fact that his past mistakes seem to have no bearing on his present behavior. If trapped while committing some unlawful act, he will often lie, excuse himself, or put the blame on someone or something else. The psychopath, in a word, is amazing. He is able to lie to others and to himself with such confidence that even the most incredible stories he relates seem to be believable.

The characteristics of the psychopath can be summed up as follows:

1. He lacks guilt.
2. He is usually bright.
3. He doesn't appear tense.
4. He is irresponsible and impulsive.
5. He cannot form personal relations—is interested only in himself.
6. He is unable to learn from experience.
7. He has no goal in life.
8. He is able to manipulate most people, including professionals like psychologists, psychiatrists, and correction and law enforcement officers.

DYSSOCIAL REACTION

The dyssocial individual is best typified by the image of the person who is classified as a *juvenile delinquent*, or a constant troublemaker. Therefore, as the reader associates the antisocial person with the term psychopath, the dyssocial individual should be paired with the person society terms a juvenile delinquent.

The dyssocial individual is one who is having difficulty with the law because of a lack in his background. The following are some of the factors contributing to his inadequate development.

1. He was raised in a section of the city where the only apparently successful person was the criminal.
2. He was reared in a structural (small and independent) society where people made their own laws—laws which in many instances showed a disregard for the social norms of the rest of society.
3. He had a family background which lent itself to the production of a person oblivious to the laws of society. In other words, to use a timeworn phrase, dyssocial individuals are "products of their environment."

Since there is no one cause for delinquency, three background factors will be discussed briefly. These are:

1. Family background
2. Neighborhood influence
3. Psychological and physical needs

As the reader can see, these are but another way of viewing the three contributing factors just mentioned above. They have been stated in a new way to facilitate a clearer presentation.

INADEQUATE FAMILY BACKGROUND

Inadequate family background is the result of an incomplete home, that is, a home where one or more of the following situations were present:

1. Father and mother were divorced or separated.
2. Father or mother were not usually at home.
3. Father or mother rejected the child.
4. Father or mother were inadequate models for the child.

More than 80 percent of the addicts from New York who were seen by this author had incomplete homes as defined by the four criteria above. The incidence of cases in which the father was totally absent or rarely present was extremely high, as was the number of cases where the child was rejected.

Rejection usually has a great impact on the adolescent. The following account is a composite of information related to the author by a number of addicts during conversations with them several years prior to this writing. It points up how rejection can be recognized quite easily by the child or adolescent.

My father and I have nothing in common, nothing! Even when I was a little kid he seemed to just tolerate me 'cause my mother had me and he couldn't dump me without hurting her. Anyway, he ignored me up to a few years ago when I entered high school. When I got with what was going on, he stopped ignoring me and started hating me. Just 'cause I wore clothes like everybody else in the crowd he treated me like a queer bum, so I figured finally, "What's the sense?" and did my thing. . . . After I got busted for acid he seemed to change his tune. I guess he felt sorta guilty. Anyway, he said he wanted me to hang around more, but when I did, it was nuthin'—we didn't have anything in common, but then we never did.

One factor, noted above, that makes a home incomplete for a child is when one or both of the parents is an inadequate model. In such a case, the child lacks someone to set an example for him to follow. The following description by a child of his stepfather gives a common illustration of a parent who was inadequate and shows one possible effect that could result from such a circumstance.

He always came home drunk. Why my mother stayed with the bum I'll never know. I figured "screw it" and left home to make it alone. I hooked with a bunch that knew how to make bread easy. . . . It makes me laugh to think about the first time I got busted. He threw a fit. And when he blew up I told him, "Who the heck are you to give me a hard time—a bum alky like you?" . . . Was he surprised when I hit him! . . .

So an incomplete home in any of the forms discussed above can indeed affect the development of a child in an adverse manner. Therefore, it must be listed as one of the primary factors in the cause of delinquency.

NEIGHBORHOOD INFLUENCE AND DELINQUENCY

The influence of a neighborhood on an individual can stem from the presence of a family organization active in criminal pursuits or from certain accepted norms in sections of the ghetto.

The effect of a family organization is illustrated well in the book and movie *The Godfather*. Early in this story there is an episode in which an individual whose daughter was assaulted seeks revenge against the youths who were involved. Dissatisfied with the action of the courts, he turns to the "godfather" for justice.

Though fictional, the full account of what transpired between the girl's father and the godfather demonstrates how a family organization might take the law into its own hands. Moreover, it shows how a youth brought up in this type of environment could easily learn that spurning the legal law enforcement agencies in favor of family action is a good which is to be emulated rather than shunned.

The norms of sections of the ghetto, though not as rigid as the rules of a family organization, may have a similar effect on a youth brought up in such an area. Often the informal rules in an environment such as this differ from—or are in direct opposition to—those of the society as a whole. The influence of a segment of a particular neighborhood could then indeed be dangerous.

PSYCHOLOGICAL AND PHYSICAL NEEDS

Ghetto philosophy arises to a great extent from the dire poverty that exists there—poverty which inflicts psychological and physical pain on those who dwell in such an environment. In some areas of the city, due to a lack of financial wealth, there exist below-standard housing, a lack of nutritious, appetizing food, a shortage of general luxuries, and almost an absence of available free-time activities. On the other hand, residents in more affluent areas at least have the economical capacity to obtain such necessities for healthy living. Thus, this unequal distribution of wealth, combined with the fact that all people have similar needs eventually, logically leads to an atmosphere of frustration in the ghetto.

HOMICIDE

Data on sociopaths as well as "normal" persons involved in homicide are now available. The general composite profile produced by the findings of most recent studies indicates that murderers usually can be described as follows:

1. They are not fully aware of the severity of the act of homicide.
2. They come from a background that was deprived either socially or economically, or both.
3. They have been subjected to a previous environment in which aggression was an accepted means of handling problems (frustration).
4. They have a low frustration tolerance.
5. They are individuals who knew the victim before the crime was committed.

Point 5 listed above is particularly interesting, since many people view the typical murderer as a heartless stranger. This is far from the case. The findings of two studies included in a report[1] by the President's Commission on Law Enforcement and Administration of Justice support the position that killings by strangers represent the minority of listed homicides. For example, the Uniform Crime Report states that in 1965 killings within the family made up 31 percent of all murders.

Another point brought out by the President's Commission was that homicide also involved—on a percentage basis—more Negroes than whites and that murders were committed more frequently by someone of the same race as the victim. The commission findings on the victim-offender relationship can be summed up as follows: A victim will usually be murdered in his own "home tract," by someone he knows, and by someone of his own race.

In addition, as the homicide rate rises, the serious forms of sexual

[1] *Crime in America: The Challenge of Crime in a Free Society*, Report by the President's Commission on Law Enforcement and Administration of Justice, U.S. Government Printing Office, Washington, 1967.

violence are also growing at an alarming rate, thus drawing the public's attention to the relationship of sexually deviant behavior to criminal assault.

SEXUAL DEVIATION

Sexually deviant behavior is that activity by a person which affords him sexual pleasure but which is deemed inappropriate by a social group or groups. Therefore, classifying areas for presentation under the topic of sexual deviance is difficult, because many techniques of sexual gratification considered inappropriate by one culture or community may simultaneously be deemed acceptable by others. For example, masturbation is viewed as an acceptable sexual outlet by a number of people in the world today, whereas there is a sizeable number who feel the opposite. In the United States polygamy is incorrect; in other parts of the world it's viewed as normal. And so, in a discussion of sexual deviation this factor must be understood.

The scope of this section on sexual deviance will include a description of fifteen types of deviation. The purpose will not be to cover the causes of the specific deviations, which would be beyond the scope of this text, but to provide enough information so that the reader is able to associate the terminology with the condition. In other words, if a professional report says that an individual is a necrophiliac, after completing this section the reader should be aware of what such a label implies.

The fifteen types of deviation which will be covered are:

1. Masturbation
2. Homosexuality
3. Satyriasis
4. Impotence
5. Prostitution
6. Incest
7. Pedophilia
8. Bestiality
9. Rape
10. Sadism
11. Masochism
12. Fetishism
13. Exhibitionism
14. Voyeurism
15. Necrophilia

Masturbation is an act in which the person stimulates his genitals as a method of achieving sexual gratification. Though this is one of the most practiced methods used by men and women prior to marriage, it is considered deviant today by society as a whole. This picture has started to change, however, as medical and psychological authorities have begun to report that it is a normal sexual outlet under most circumstances.

Homosexuality is present when two members of the same gender are involved in sexual relations with each other.

In the prison setting, homosexual activities are common among adolescents. An adolescent might seek to rape a fellow inmate, not only because he's more aware of his drive than an adult prisoner, but also because of the status involved. The adolescent prison culture looks upon homosexual rape as an episode in which a person can demonstrate that he is strong. The victim is seen as a weak homosexual, even if he was overcome by force, whereas the rapist is viewed as strong since he was the dominant partner, playing the male role.

Satyriasis is a term used to describe the condition of a male who is involved in excessive sexual activity; *nymphomania* is the same condition in a female. Naturally, since the word "excessive" is subject to many interpretations, it would be difficult to apply either classification to someone unless the individual's daily activities were all concerned with sexual pleasure.

Impotence is present when a man has difficulty in achieving sexual gratification or does not have a desire to reach it. The female counterpart is *frigidity*, which is more common than impotence. According to Coleman:[2]

> For both impotence and frigidity, the only effective means of correction is usually the establishment of a stable, intimate, affectionate relationship involving confidence, security, and love.

Prostitution is the giving of sexual gratification in exchange for a fee. Promiscuity would be the same as prostitution but for the absence of a monetary reward. As in prostitution, the sexual relationship is formed casually, probably without prior knowledge of the sexual partners.

Incest occurs when sexual relations take place between members of the same family—i.e., mother and son, father and daughter, brother and sister. Of all the above combinations, incest occurs more frequently between brothers and sisters, especially when for some reason children of the opposite sex are forced to sleep in the same bed after puberty.

Pedophilia is the term given to a sexual relationship in which one of the partners is a child. Pedophiliacs are commonly referred to as child molesters. It is of interest to note that Kinsey and a number of

---

[2] James C. Coleman, *Abnormal Psychology and Modern Life*, Scott, Foresman, Glenville, Ill., 1965, p. 385.

other researchers have found that children often misinterpret the affections of an older person as being sexual, especially in these times of increased crime. Furthermore, other researchers have indicated that often the child is more than passively involved in the act, sometimes in fact seducing the older person into becoming sexually aroused.

A study by De Francis also pointed out the following concerning the "typical" sexual offender:

> The stereotype of the sexual offender against children is the pervert who lurks at a schoolyard to lure a child into his car. This does happen. But such cases are in the minority. In 75 percent of the cases, the offender is a member of the child's own household, a neighbor, a friend, or a person in the community with whom the child has frequent contact.[3]

Bestiality is the reference used when a sexual act takes place with an animal. This does not occur very often today; it is present to some degree, however, in rural areas of the country.

Rape is well known to those in law enforcement because of its increasing occurrence—especially in urban areas. In rape, a normal sexual act takes place under abnormal conditions (this of course excludes statutory rape). It is of interest to note that when one thinks of rape, it is often associated with physical harm being done to the victim. This is just not true. Figures indicate that approximately 4 to 6 percent of convicted sex offenders were responsible for inflicting bodily harm upon their victims. Moreover, sex offenders represent a low recidivism rate among the prison population. Only about 10 percent of those sex offenders now incarcerated have been confined previously for similar offenses. The author brings out these two points because the popular, but inaccurate, notions held by many people concerning sex offenders are that they usually inflict physical harm on their victims and that they are "repeaters." Statistics tend to disprove both ideas.

According to one study (Gebhard, Gagnon, Pomeroy, and Christenson), the majority of rapists can be described as "criminally involved men who take what they want, whether money, material, or women, and their sex offenses are by-products of their general criminality."[4]

---

[3] Vincent De Francis, "Protecting the Child Victim of Sex Crimes Committed by Adults." *Federal Probation*, vol. 35, no. 3, September 1971, p. 17.

[4] Donald R. Cressy and David A. Ward (eds.), *Delinquency, Crime, and Social Process*, Harper and Row, New York, 1969, p. 1073.

Sadism and *masochism* are often in the news. Sadism is a term which usually refers to the infliction of pain by one individual on another for the purpose of receiving sexual pleasure. (However, it can also mean merely the application of cruel treatment in order to attain nonsexual enjoyment.) Masochism is the deviant complement of sadism. It is present in a person who derives sexual gratification from being subjected to pain.

Fetishism is the concentration of attention on some object or some section of the anatomy for sexual purposes. Such objects can include stockings, bras, and panties, for example. Or they might be parts of the body, like the legs, breasts, or the nape of the neck. The individual who is deeply involved in fetishism may caress, kiss, or masturbate on the object. *Kleptomaniacs*, who steal compulsively, will often take objects for sexual gratification.

Exhibitionism and *voyeurism* are two other types of sexual deviance. Exhibitionism is the attainment of sexual pleasure by exposing one's genitals in a public place; voyeurism describes the actions of a "peeping Tom" who becomes sexually excited through secretly viewing a member of the opposite sex undress, engage in intercourse, or perform some act of a sexual nature.

The last type of sexual deviance to be included in this chapter is the rare abnormality called *necrophilia*. A necrophiliac is an individual who receives sexual pleasure from viewing or having intercourse with a female corpse. This extreme form of deviance is associated with severely psychologically ill individuals. The chances are that the reader will have no contact in his lifetime with an individual of this type.

LAW ENFORCEMENT AND CORRECTION OFFICERS AND THE PSYCHOPATH

As can be surmised from what was said in this chapter about the psychopath (antisocial person) and the dyssocial individual, handling people who fit into these categories can be dangerous. Yet, as in the case of any classification of abnormality, identifying someone who fits into a particular category of aberrant behavior is almost impossible without the aid of professional assistance.

However, three basic points concerning often-found traits in psychopathic and dyssocial persons can be reiterated here. If anything, they should convince the officer that he must not rely on his common sense alone when judging an individual, for from the following statements one can see how excellent a liar and manipulator such a person can be.

In essence then, these types of criminals:

1. Are especially convincing deceivers, since their lack of guilt permits them to remain calm when being interrogated about a crime they have committed.
2. Have no (or very little) feeling about violently lashing out at an officer or citizen if it means escape from capture.
3. Are so impulsive that they may try anything on the spur of the moment when confronted by someone while committing a crime.

And so, because of the deceptive, dangerous nature of psychopaths and most dyssocial persons, instead of using common sense one must maintain some degree of wary attentiveness when dealing with any suspect. To be completely surprised by an apparently innocent suspect is something than an officer can ill afford.

Similarly, in the case of the correction officer, handling prisoners puts him into contact with a relatively high number of these individuals. Accordingly, though the officer should afford them consideration as fellow human beings, he must also be alert to the possibility that the prisoner is trying to manipulate him through some word or gesture.

Despite the fact that such warnings about possible psychopaths to the law enforcement and correction officer may seem dramatic, they are unfortunately quite necessary in view of the fact that officers must deal with so many antisocial persons.

WHAT WAS COVERED IN THIS CHAPTER

In this chapter on sociopathic personality disturbances, antisocial and dyssocial reactions were discussed. In addition, different types of sexual deviance were presented so that the reader can understand deviant terminology if he comes across it in professional literature or on the job.

In the discussion of antisocial individuals, the psychopath was cited as a person who:

1. Lacks guilt
2. Is usually bright
3. Doesn't appear tense
4. Is irresponsible
5. Cannot form personal relations

6. Is unable to learn from experience
7. Has no goals in life
8. Is able to manipulate most people

In describing the dyssocial person, the effects of inadequate family background, neighborhood influence, and psychological and physical needs were stressed to show their part in causing the spread of delinquency.

In the section on sexual deviance, emphasis was placed on the fact that what is considered deviant is ultimately determined by the social norms of the culture or community. It was pointed out that studies on child molesting show that the offender and victim usually know each other. Ironically, this is also true in the case of homicide.

This chapter, covering the antisocial and dyssocial person as well as the sexual deviant, was meant then as an introduction to some of the various reactions which can be subsumed under the category of sociopathic disorders. The other disorders in this group, namely alcoholism and drug addiction, will be discussed in Chapters 7 and 8.

REVIEW

1. From what does a character disorder result?
2. What is another name for an antisocial individual?
3. Give eight characteristics of a psychopath.
4. What three contributing causes of juvenile delinquency were discussed in this chapter?
5. Define the following terms:

Satyriasis	Sadism
Impotence	Masochism
Incest	Fetishism
Pedophilia	Exhibitionism
Bestiality	Voyeurism

6. What two popular notions concerning sexual offenders were noted to be false?

chapter seven

Alcoholism

Alcoholism is a problem. Practically everyone knows this. Yet many people don't realize that it's actually a mammoth health problem. It is estimated that there are 9 million alcoholics in this country alone! Among federal civil employees the estimated annual cost of alcoholism in the federal government is between $275 million and $550 million. Alcoholism programs in the federal government could save from $135 million to $280 million a year. Losses in industry because of alcoholism have been computed at $10 billion per year. One in every thirteen employees is an alcoholic. The total cost to the nation, and the human loss to individuals, families, and communities, are incalculable.

In addition, alcoholism has had a particularly strong impact on the law enforcement scene. The Federal Bureau of Investigation reports that one out of every three arrests involves alcohol abuse; approximately one-half of all fatal accidents today involve an alcoholic; over 90 percent of *short-term* prisoners are confined because of their contact with alcohol; suicide is committed by alcoholics as compared with nonalcoholics at a ratio of 58 to 1. Since alcoholism poses such tremendous problems for those concerned with law enforcement, an officer should understand more about the disorder and how to deal with it.

BRIEF HISTORICAL BACKGROUND

No one knows who discovered alcohol, but it has evidently been with us since the beginning of recorded history. In addition to its use for the sake of the euphoria it provides, alcohol has also played an integral part in religious or ritualistic ceremonies as far back as historians can trace.

As early as 4000 B.C. wine and beer were present in Egypt. In China, around 1100 B.C., laws were being imposed in connection with alcohol's sale and consumption. According to the Bible, wine was present during the time of the Old Testament.

During the medieval period in Europe, alcohol was consumed frequently to the extent that it became part of the daily routine. European acceptance of its role in religious ceremonies and as an aid to help one meet the day-to-day pressures of life was carried over the sea to the New World. In colonial America, not only was alcohol used on holidays, it was fashionable for it to be served at meals and social affairs and to be provided for travelers who stopped for lodging, food, and drink.

In America, the marketing of spirits has always been part of the economy. Alcohol's use in the past has set the stage for the incredibly large quantity of liquor consumed today in the United States and the rest of the world. The present generation is continuing this trend to the extent that tomorrow's population will be subject to the same, if not more, pressure to continue emptying the bottle and the cask. And this can only mean that alcoholism will be on the increase; alcoholics will swell in number.

WHAT IS ALCOHOLISM?

Alcoholism is a disease. It is a progressive disease—one that can get worse if not properly treated. However, unlike a disease such as syphilis, which is contracted through body contact, alcoholism is spread as a result of ignorance and inattention. Therefore, preventive measures must be taken to ensure that its bounding growth is stunted by means of education on the nature of alcoholism, on how it can be detected, and on methods of treatment when someone is enslaved by it.

Alcoholism can be considered a psychological, physiological, and social problem. Persons suffering from it use alcohol repeatedly and excessively. This uncontrollable intake of alcohol leads to an upheaval in the drinker's social and economic status. He alienates both his family and friends. His life is centered on drinking to such a great extent that:

1. He spends little time with those close to him.
2. His personality is altered under the influence of alcohol.
3. His health is being adversely affected to the extent that he is often laid up at home or in the hospital due to an internal problem, such as cirrhosis of the liver, or to an accident, such as falling down a flight of stairs while inebriated.

These difficulties can be further complicated by his poor work habits. On the job he often performs well below capacity. He has a tendency to be continually late and can never be relied on when a problem arises since he is notorious for absenteeism and works poorly under any kind of stress-producing conditions. Combine these liabilities with his sometimes unappealing personal appearance and his inability to work at a reasonable pace, and the alcoholic proves to be an employee no one wants—especially at a decent wage. Even if he does manage to get a job, a good deal of his salary is spent over the bar or in a liquor store. So usually when someone falls prey to alcoholism, the family suffers as much as the individual himself does.

Alcoholism, in summary, is:

1. A progressive disease
2. A psychological, physiological, and social problem
3. A condition in which someone uses alcohol repeatedly and excessively without being able to control it
4. A disorder which usually causes an upheaval in the drinker's social and economic status

Consequently, alcoholism is a dreaded problem, and there are no easy answers to the question "Who is an alcoholic?"

WHO IS AN ALCOHOLIC?

People have described alcoholics in a multitude of ways ever since this disease has been known. The alcoholic has been called selfish, immature, insecure, irresponsible, and, by some people, a latent homosexual. Today, as society increasingly searches for labels for everything and everyone, those interested in alcoholism are looking for a pat description of the alcoholic.

Until quite recently the popular notion of an alcoholic as a skid row bum, a sloppy, filthy, red-eyed, shaky character, was accepted as a true description of the "typical" sufferer. Now we realize that for 95 percent of all alcoholics this view simply is not valid. When an individual is under the influence of an excessive quantity of alcohol, he may present an image similar to that of the "skid row drunk," but in the main—especially when sober—he is not distinguishable from the nonalcoholic.

Is there anything that can be said about the alcoholic, then, to determine a little more about him? Yes, a number of facts have been gathered. However, the composite picture put together by these statistics does not give us a model which will fit all, or even most, alcoholics. With this in mind consider some general comments that can be made about alcoholics.

1. Men make up the bulk of alcoholics in the country today.
2. The incidence of alcoholism is higher among certain nationalities (e.g., Irish and French) than in others (e.g., Italians and Jews).
3. Certain personality traits are more prevalent in the alcoholic population than among nonalcoholics.
4. On the whole, alcoholics are in their middle age.

In looking at the above conclusions, one can see that researchers don't appear to be any closer to answering the question "Who is an alcoholic?" than they were before, when it was thought that alcoholics were found only on skid row.

Even though no particular personality pattern classification can be assigned to the alcoholic other than general application of the terminology of a character disorder, there are a number of personality inadequacies which appear frequently in most alcoholics. They are:

1. Insecurity
2. Immaturity
3. Overdependency
4. Loneliness
5. Sexual inadequacy

All the above traits are usually present to some degree in alcoholics, though they differ in intensity. For example, many alcoholics with adult responsibilities face life as a young teenager would. This immaturity is often caused by the individual's insecurity due to a real or imagined deficiency in his intelligence, appearance, physical prowess, ability to socialize, or a combination of these attributes. In a sizable number of cases both this insecurity and immaturity were manifested in youth by an overdependency in their relationships with others, especially with those of the opposite sex. This inability to adapt to the demands of adulthood might have caused the individual to become hypersensitive to criticism and disapproval.

The answer to these problems and a way of removing surface tension and anxiety was slowly—sometimes abruptly—sought in a bottle, at a bar, or on a table in a lounge.

Naturally, this oversimplifies the personality design of the alcoholic, but despite the marginal errors that come with simplification, it is felt that these types of personality inadequacies are so prevalent in a number of alcoholics today that to exclude them from this chapter would be a mistake.

To add to the above description of the alcoholic, the steps leading to alcoholism should be considered.

STEPS LEADING TO ALCOHOLISM

Some individuals seem destined to be alcoholics. They take their first drink, and within months they have reached the ultimate stage of alcoholism. However, most individuals take longer to do so; some even manage to remain in society indefinitely, cleverly avoiding discovery although they are alcoholics in the full sense of the word. This is unfortunate, because the earlier the disease of alcoholism is spotted, the sooner treatment can begin. Some alcoholics sneak drinks and carefully discard bottles all their life, only to waste their best years in this pursuit.

When an individual becomes an alcoholic, he usually goes through a number of stages or steps, though they blend together differently for each particular person.

Step One: The New Drinker

This step is the beginning. The first drink is taken for social, religious, or other reasons. After this initial contact with alcohol, the person *not* headed for alcoholism usually remains at this step. He takes an occasional drink and even at times drinks a bit too much. However, when this occurs, he experiences a "hangover" the following morning which is accompanied by the feeling that he never wants to see another drink "for a million years!"

Step Two: Warning Signs—Heavy Drinking and "Blackouts"

At this point the individual is drinking more and more at parties or the local tavern. He finds that the euphoria he receives from drinking is especially pleasurable. It seems only logical to him that he should enjoy fully the relief and enjoyment that drinking can provide.

It is at this step that the onset of "blackouts" appears. By "blackouts" it is not meant that he drinks himself into oblivion, but that on the following morning after drinking heavily, he doesn't remember what happened after a certain point in the evening. The realization that this has occurred can often bring about feelings of remorse, especially in women; or sometimes these blackouts seem to the drinker to be half amusing.

Step Three: Extra Drinking Required

Before the individual goes out to a party, a friend's house, or a lounge he frequents, he usually starts the night off early by taking several drinks. Doing this helps him to get "high" more easily when he begins drinking later. What's happening here is twofold. The drinker is building up a tolerance for alcohol, and he is becoming self-conscious about his drinking. He is finding it harder and harder to feel the drinks he gulps down. At this stage he is paradoxically *anxious about alcohol not removing his anxiety*. Simultaneously, since more alcohol is necessary to bring about the desirable effect and others are beginning to notice his increased heavy drinking, he begins sneaking drinks.

During this period of development the drinker has started to realize that drinking is important to his well-being. Without it he believes life will not be as full for him. When visiting friends or attending social gatherings he becomes concerned about whether there will be enough to drink there of the "right stuff" (hard liquor rather than wine).

Step Four: Losing One's Grip on Alcohol

On this level the individual can control when he will drink, but not how much he will consume. So to some extent one can say that he has not lost complete control of his drinking behavior; however, if he does begin to drink, his willpower becomes muted. When dropping in at a bar for a few or going out to a party he may tell himself that he will have only a few tonight because tomorrow's a big day for him at the office. Yet telling himself is as far as it gets, because once he starts drinking he can't stop until he has become really intoxicated.

Step Five: Excuse Drinking

At this stage the individual is continually excusing his drinking behavior to himself and others. Often during this period he will go without drinking for days, weeks or sometimes even months. Having convinced himself he can stay away from it, he begins drinking again. When he starts back on the road to heavy intake of alcohol, he uses whatever excuses are available to him (birthday, weekend, getting away from it all, etc.). In addition, when the amount he drinks is considerable and he gets quite inebriated, he has excuses for this as well (tired, been under stress recently, drank without eating). These excuses are a cover for the increasing guilt that he feels about his drinking behavior and his gnawing worry that the alcohol is controlling him rather than the other way round.

Step Six: Drinking Alone

Drinking alone is a logical progression from step 5, excuse drinking. The individual at this level feels that people are too critical of his drinking behavior. Furthermore, he believes that alcohol gives him a special sense of pleasure when he sits alone with a drink by his side. Also, when drinking by himself he can move quickly and undisturbed into a world of fantasy. This fantasy world can revolve around many desires, such as the type of work he'd like to do, the women he'd like to be with, or the kind of man he feels he would truly like to be. Unfortunately, since he is wasting all his energy and time drinking and dreaming, he has even less chance of attaining his goals than if he were sober. This he knows, and it contributes to making his situation worse.

Step Seven: Antisocial Drinker

Just as drinking alone is a logical offshoot of excuse drinking, becoming antisocial in a demonstrative way is a natural progression from the habit of lone drinking, in which the individual is shunning society and drawing within himself. In this stage, the person gets into unwarranted fights with members of his family as well as strangers. He is full of hostility. He becomes destructive and shows no apparent concern for those whom he should love. At this step the drinker can start to become an almost daily resident of the local jail and a familiar face to the policemen in the area.

Step Eight: New Hangover

On this step, which really meshes with the previous three, the person treats his hangover the following morning differently from the normal social drinker. Whereas the social drinker (step 1) would avoid any contact with alcohol if he had side effects from drinking the previous night, the person on this step would "bite the animal that bit him" and take another drink. This method of treating his hangover leads into another session of drinking which will last until he goes to sleep again that evening. In other words, the alcoholic drinks in the morning to treat his hangover and doesn't stop until he retires at night. This process leads into step 9.

Step Nine: "Benders"

Benders are extended periods of drinking. At this stage the alcoholic becomes obvious to those around him. Up to this point, many alcoholics remain hidden and thus regrettably avoid treatment. During this period the person on a bender will typify the so-called skid row alcoholic. He is oblivious to personal safety, health, comfort, or his family's welfare. Occasionally this step can be a motivating force for the alcoholic to seek help when he sobers up.

Step Ten: Hitting Bottom

This is the last phase. By the time the alcoholic has reached this step, he has suffered great mental and physical anguish. He has a choice at this point—and it may be his last. The alcoholic can continue to drink and can end up going through a maze of diseases and accidents to reach a sorry death, or he can seek help. Regrettable as it may seem, many alcoholics reach this stage before seeking help, and some seek it when it is too late.

TREATMENT FOR THE ALCOHOLIC

Alcoholism can be caused by a number of factors, and it affects each individual in a particular way. Therefore there is no one specific way in which an alcoholic can be rehabilitated. Numerous techniques have been tried. Since they cannot all be enumerated here, only four of the most important methods will be discussed. They are·

1. Psychotherapy
2. Hospital outpatient treatment
3. Conditioned reflex treatment
4. Fellowship and spiritual renewal

With psychotherapy the primary goal is to get the alcoholic to make an initial behavior change as well as to alter his basic attitude toward life and drinking. This technique is employed by a trained counselor, psychologist, or psychiatrist. It is sometimes a lengthy procedure. It requires concentration on the alcoholic's personality problems, which seemingly are not connected with his alcoholism. The basic thinking here is that alcoholism is a behavioral outgrowth of problems that lie deeper and that these problems must be treated if the alcoholic is to be effectively rehabilitated.

Hospital outpatient treatment can supply excellent treatment services. In addition to the medical attention given to the diseases and malnutrition that accompany alcoholism, outpatient departments often provide psychotherapy, occupation therapy, and recreation facilities for the alcoholic. It is usually this agency that uses the conditioned reflex treatment.

Conditioned reflex treatment is administered chiefly with the use of drugs and electrical shocks. This method was briefly discussed in an earlier chapter on conditioning. The drug Antabuse is given to the alcoholic so that he will experience an adverse reaction to drinking; this in turn will condition the individual to withdraw from alcohol rather than be drawn to it. Shocks administered when the alcoholic takes a drink—or, in the case of a problem drinker, when he drinks too much too fast—cause him to avoid drinking because of the painful reaction he receives. Since this method is based on the cooperation of the alcoholic, it has some obvious shortcomings. However, the advantage of Antabuse is that its effects last five to seven days after its use has been discontinued.

Despite the facility and effectiveness of the previous three methods, the fourth one to be described is by far the most famous and effective. This of course is the technique employed by Alcoholics Anonymous, or A.A., as it is commonly called. A.A. was founded by a doctor and an alcoholic who had stopped drinking. It has made incredible strides in helping alcoholics. Since its inception it has aided hundreds of thousands of alcoholics to return to sober, more productive lives. A.A. is based on a sense of fellowship, spirituality, and personal commitment. The organization has twelve steps and twelve traditions which the alcoholic should subscribe to if he desires to be successful in his fight against the bottle. To get a feeling for A.A.'s philosophy, look over the *Twelve Steps of Alcoholics Anonymous:*

1. We admitted we were powerless over alcohol—that our lives had become unmanageable.

2. Came to believe that a Power greater than ourselves could restore us to sanity.
3. Made a decision to turn our will and our lives over to the care of God *as we understood Him.*
4. Made a searching and fearless moral inventory of ourselves.
5. Admitted to God, to ourselves, and to another human being the exact nature of our wrongs.
6. Were entirely ready to have God remove all these defects of character.
7. Humbly asked Him to remove our shortcomings.
8. Made a list of all persons we had harmed, and became willing to make amends to them all.
9. Made direct amends to such people whenever possible, except when to do so would injure them or others.
10. Continued to take personal inventory, and when we were wrong, promptly admitted it.
11. Sought through prayer and meditation to improve our conscious contact with God, *as we understood Him*, praying only for knowledge of His will for us and the power to carry that out.
12. Having had a spiritual awakening as the result of these steps, we tried to carry this message to alcoholics and to practice these principles in all our affairs.[1]

As can be gathered from these steps, A.A. seeks to get the alcoholic to reflect on his past, take action to correct himself, and gradually return to society. This approach, based on a nonspecific theology, has proved to date to be the most effective large-scale technique for dealing with the problem of alcoholism. At the very least, and without doing it full justice, the work of A.A. can be described as commendable.

SPREADING THE WORD ABOUT ALCOHOLISM

There are a number of organizations involved in the treatment of alcoholics, and it is impossible to mention them all. The author concentrated above on Alcoholics Anonymous. The same principle applies to the area of education about alcoholism. There are many private and governmental organizations involved in educational services for the purpose of disseminating information on alcoholism and

[1] Reprinted by permission of A.A. World Services, Inc.

problem drinking. However, the one private organization that stands out above all is the National Council on Alcoholism, or NCA.

The NCA supplements the great work that A.A. does. It effectively performs numerous much-needed functions in the fight against alcoholism. Some of them are:

1. Assembling facts and literature on alcoholism which can be understood by the layman
2. Widely disseminating information in this field
3. Sparking action and public opinion on the problem of alcoholism

In pursuit of these goals their success has been overwhelming.

It is essential that the reader be aware of this organization's function and its location (2 Park Avenue, New York, N.Y. 10016), because by contacting its staff through the mail or visiting their library at headquarters he can be in touch with the latest and most complete sources of information on the subject of alcoholism available today. A law enforcement officer deals quite often with the problem of alcoholism. If he would like to do further research in this area, NCA is the organization to contact.

DRINKING AND DRIVING

Driving while under the influence of alcohol has presented a deathly problem for pedestrians and drivers alike since the invention of the "horseless carriage." Even before that time drinking caused difficulties. In England a justice of the peace accused drunken mothers of allowing their children to dash about without supervision, thus causing accidents to horses and carriages. So the trouble caused—directly or indirectly—by those who drink has been present since people started driving.

However, the dangers brought on by mixing alcohol with gasoline have not been heeded even though they have accounted for a majority of traffic fatalities among drivers and pedestrians. It seems incredible that motorists would blatantly defy the statistics. The answer to this puzzling situation may be found in the "not me" syndrome. Most drivers who drink do not get into accidents. Because they have been fortunate to date, they feel that the facts listed by the National Safety Council do not apply to them. As a result, they feel that driving home from a party or local tavern after drinking excessively is fine *for them*.

What they don't realize is that up to this point they've simply been lucky! Tomorrow their luck may run out, and death or serious injury will prove to them too late that they can become a statistic as well.

Drivers who "don't feel drunk" fail to realize that as few as two drinks can cause

1. Impaired judgment
2. Distorted vision
3. Unrealistic self-image
4. Slowed reaction time

These shortcomings may not be noticed by the driver, but they are present.

As a matter of fact it has become a medico-legal puzzle to determine whether a person is too inebriated to drive. Two developments have caused the situation to become clearer. One was a 1935 decision by the Arizona Supreme Court which has been endorsed by the American Medical Association and the National Safety Council.

> The expression "under the influence of intoxicating liquor" covers not only all the well-known and easily recognizable conditions and degrees of intoxication, but also any abnormal mental or physical condition which is the result of indulging to any degree in intoxicating liquors and which tends to deprive the individual of that clearness of intellect and control of himself which he would otherwise possess. If the ability of the driver of an automobile has been lessened in the slightest degree by the use of intoxicating liquors, then the driver is deemed to be under the influence of intoxicating liquor. The mere fact that a driver has taken a drink does not place him under the ban of the statute unless such drink has some influence upon him, lessening in some degree his ability to handle said automobile.[2]

This decision has been interpreted by most states to the effect that:

1. Less than 0.05 percent alcohol level in the blood means no intoxication.
2. Between 0.05 and 0.15 percent alcohol level in the blood indicates the individual may be under the influence of alcohol.
3. Over 0.15 percent alcohol level in the blood is prima facie evidence that the person is intoxicated.

[2] *Steffani v. State*, 45 orig. 210. 42P. 2d 615(1936), p. 618.

The second major development was in 1953 in New York, when the "implied consent law" was put into effect.[3] Under this law it is understood that when a motorist receives a permit to drive, he agrees to submit to a chemical test when a law enforcement officer requests him to or he will lose his license. Under this act the driver is bound to be tested to see whether he is under the influence of alcohol if the police deem it necessary.

However, no matter how efficient the enforcement of driving regulations, if the courts do not prosecute the drunken offender, nothing is accomplished. Recently there has been an intensive campaign in most areas of the country to deal firmly with persons who drive while under the influence. Therefore, the motorist may still take a chance on driving after drinking, but he is aware of the grim consequences. This does not seem to be much consolation for the pedestrian and the safe driver, in that the laws have no deterrent effect. Yet, if the motorist who drinks is taken off the road through suspension of his license, at least the odds will be lessened against meeting an intoxicated driver.

HANDLING THE ALCOHOLIC

Merely to understand the problem of alcoholism, important as it is, is not enough to satisfy a professional law enforcement officer. The peace officer must deal almost every day with those under the influence and should therefore know how to handle them. With this objective in mind the Smithers Foundation published *Alcohol and Alcoholism: A Police Handbook.* The following material is quoted from the section therein on "Handling the Intoxicated Person or Alcoholic."

In handling the "drunk" or alcoholic in your course of duty as a police officer, you will encounter many different problems. Knowing how to handle these could, in some cases, mean the difference between life and death. Your very first problem will be to determine the extent of drunkenness. You must decide whether the person is in such a state as to be capable of hurting himself or others. If he does seem potentially dangerous, then he must be taken into custody, or at least protected.

With the sleepy, depressed type, you must be especially careful. He may appear quite capable of sleeping off his current state of

---

[3] New York Vehicle and Traffic Law of 1929, Sec. 71(a), as added by L.1953, c.854.

intoxication. But he may have downed a pint or more of whiskey, or some such drink, just before you arrested him—in which case, he will get more and more intoxicated in the following hour or two. If left alone in a cell and not watched, he could die from the absorption of extra alcohol during that time. So your second problem involves your ability to recognize some of the common danger signs and complications of severe intoxication.

Possible Complications:

Coma—Initially the victim is drowsy, very sad, and sick. He may be aggressive when disturbed. Later he may develop some definite physical signs, such as skin pallor. Looking at him you will see his eyes crossed or pointing out. He may complain of ringing in his ears, numbness "all over," and seeing double. His pulse becomes rapid, the eye pupils—tiny in the first stage—now become very large. Later he goes into increasing stupor, from which it is difficult to arouse him, and he may die of one of two things:

Shock—signs are paleness, sweating, clammy skin, fainting, and weak pulse;

Total anesthesia of the brain—this could happen within two or three hours of first seeing a drunken person.

Convulsions—These are a possibly frightening, possibly dangerous development of the hangover stage. The immediate dangers are that the victim may fall and hurt himself or that his airway may become blocked, so-called swallowing of the tongue. The general danger is that the convulsion may indicate a very serious medical condition. The best treatment is to lay the convulsive patient on his back, if possible, loosen any tight clothing, and put something soft, such as a rolled-up shirt tail, in the corner of his mouth. This will prevent him from biting his tongue and will give him an airway. After administering first aid a physician should be called, and the person should be watched until medical advice is obtained.

Alcoholic Hallucinosis—This lasts from minutes to days. The victim sees and hears things that are not really there. He is convinced that they are there, and they may be vivid, frightening, and terrifying. Sometimes he may have delusions (feeling perhaps someone is after his life). Apart from these abnormalities, however, he is rational, can talk, and knows who you are and what time of day it is. He doesn't usually have a fast pulse, fever, or tremor, and is not sweating, pale, or flushed. In fact, he looks all right, but "sees things."

Delirium Tremens—This is a serious possible complication of the hangover stage. The person suffering from delirium tremens is out of contact with his surroundings and does not know what is going on, though there may be clear periods. You may wear a uniform, but he will not necessarily recognize this or realize what it means. He may not know where he is, what time of day or what month it is, or even what nationality he is. He doesn't "know" anything! He often has some fever, is flushed, has a rapid pulse and intense tremor. In addition, he has the typical disturbing hallucinations and suffers from insomnia and great exhaustion. Usually the condition lasts from two to seven days. Fortunately, it is rare, but it is very serious and requires urgent medical attention.

In any of the above circumstances, after first aid is administered, if indicated, the person should be taken to the nearest medical facility.[4]

The above quote is especially important to remember since most alcoholics are processed in jail, where the fewest medical services are available, rather than in a hospital or rehabilitation center.

Another danger in dealing with alcoholics is the possibility of attempted suicide. Their suicide rate is 58 times that of nonalcoholics. Therefore, the officer should be aware of how to deal with someone threatening suicide.

An alcoholic may become severely depressed while drinking and feel that life is not worth living. If the officer does not take the person seriously, or if he makes a sudden, threatening move toward him, it might result in an unfortunate loss of life.

The following points should be applied, then, when coming into contact with a person threatening suicide:

1. Take all threats to commit suicide seriously.
2. Don't threaten someone who is threatening suicide.
3. Try to stimulate the "will to live" in the individual.
4. Don't make any sudden moves toward the person until you are close enough to grab hold of him.
5. Send someone to get professional assistance (clergyman, doctor) while you are speaking to him.

WHAT WAS COVERED IN THIS CHAPTER

Alcoholism and handling the alcoholic were focused on in this chapter. Alcoholism was noted to be:

1. A progressive disease
2. A psychological, physiological, and social problem

[4] The Correctional Association of New York and The International Association of Chiefs of Police, *Alcohol and Alcoholism: A Police Handbook*, Smithers Foundation, New York, 1965, pp. 24–26.

3. A condition in which the person suffering from it uses alcohol repeatedly and excessively without being able to control it
4. A disorder which usually causes an upheaval in the drinker's social and economic status

Ten steps to alcoholism and five personality defects often found in alcoholics were also presented in this chapter. The five personality defects were:

1. Insecurity
2. Immaturity
3. Overdependency
4. Loneliness
5. Sexual inadequacy

Treatment for alcoholics can be effected in a number of ways. The results of A.A.'s work show that fellowship and spiritual renewal seem to have the most impressive record thus far, though theirs is not the only method being used successfully today. Three other approaches mentioned were psychotherapy, hospital outpatient treatment, and conditioned reflex treatment.

As successful as A.A. has been in the treatment of alcoholics, two other organizations were cited for their work in the prevention of alcoholism through education. They were the National Council on Alcoholism and the Smithers Foundation. The NCA has been particularly active, maintaining one of the largest libraries on the subject at its headquarters in New York.

The problems encountered by those who drink and drive were also discussed. The effects two drinks can cause were listed as impaired judgment, distorted vision, unrealistic self-image, and slowed reaction time.

The final part of the chapter was devoted to the handling of alcoholic individuals. Coma, convulsions, alcoholic hallucinosis, and delirium tremens—some of the complications of alcohol abuse—were described, and five points concerning the handling of alcoholics threatening suicide were presented.

The above information on alcoholism should be regarded by the peace officer as being of the utmost importance. After all, who comes into more contact with those who drink too much than the bartender or law enforcement officer?

REVIEW

1. What is alcoholism?
2. Is the popular notion of an alcoholic which depicts him as a "skid row character" valid?
3. Name ten steps leading to alcoholism which are noted in this chapter.
4. What are the four primary types of treatment for alcoholics now in use?
5. What is NCA?
6. What is A.A.?
7. What four effects can as few as two drinks have on a person who drives?
8. What are the four possible complications resulting from abuse of alcohol which the officer should be aware of?
9. What five points should a law enforcement officer be aware of in handling a person threatening suicide?

chapter eight

Drug Addiction

In the United States drug abuse has moved swiftly, silently, and steadily from being only a bothersome problem to the point where it is now an almost epidemic horror. It is strangling our cities and corroding the suburbs—even the rural sections of the nation are no longer immune.

Law enforcement agencies are being mobilized round the clock to combat the plague of crime which drug users have initiated to support their habits. In too many cases the drug habit has created a new subculture of self-destructive adolescents who might otherwise have become productive youths. And as they enter adulthood these teenagers are spurning maturity for the futility of a drug-centered life.

The following poem, apparently written by a drug addict, is a vivid assessment of the evil potency of drug addiction. It should give the reader a realistically clear impression of how grim the situation really is and an indication of what a tremendous hold a drug can actually have over a human being. It should be read slowly and thoughtfully in order to gain the full impact of what the poet is trying to say.

King Heroin

Anonymous

Beware my friend
My name is King Heroin.
Where I come from everybody knows.
I come from the land where the poppy seeds grow.

I entered this country without a passport.
Ever since then I've been hunted and sought,
By junkies, addicts and plainclothes dicks,
But mostly by a sick junkie who needs a quick fix.

My little white grains are nothing but waste.
I'm soft and bitter and deadly to taste.
I'm worlds powerful, all know it's true,
Use me just once and you'll know it too.

I'll make a schoolboy forget about his books.
And I'll cause a world beauty to neglect her looks.
I'll make a good husband cast away his wife,
And send a greedy pusher to prison for life.

I'm king of crime, prince of corruption.
I'll capture your soul and cause your destruction.
More precious than diamonds, more treasured than gold,
My value to some is brutally told.

Ahhh! The police have taken you from under my wing.
They dare defy me, I who am King.
They have taken you from me for a short rest,
But they cannot rule me, for I am the best.

You'll curse my name and down me in speech,
But you would pick me up again if I were in reach.
At night while you're sleeping and planning your fate,
You know I'll be waiting just beyond the gate.

I gave you warning, but you didn't heed.
So put your foot in my stirrup and ride my steed.
When you ride me you'll ride me well.
On the White Horse of Heroin, you'll ride to Hell.

With this vivid picture of heroin addiction as a backdrop, an introduction to the following categories of drugs will be presented: narcotics, depressants, stimulants, hallucinogens, and volatile substances.

NARCOTICS

A narcotic is an addicting drug that induces sleep or stupor and relieves pain as a result of its depressant effect on the central nervous system (CNS). Drugs classified as narcotics are opium, opium derivatives (heroin, morphine, and codeine), and synthetic opiates (meperidine, methadone).

Opium, a dark brown substance, is the dehydrated, coagulated milk of an unripe opium poppy. As a drug it has been replaced primarily by heroin and morphine. It is taken by the user through a pipe—usually a long-stemmed one. Some of the slang terms for opium are "tar," "OP," "black stuff," and "hop."

Heroin, a white or light brown powder, is the best-known and most dangerous of the narcotic drugs. (It can be as much as ten times more potent than morphine.) Heroin can be taken by "snorting," "skin popping," or "mainlining." When a person "snorts" it, he inhales it to receive a "high," which is a sensation of euphoria. In "skin popping" the individual injects the heroin under the skin. However, these two techniques do not produce as strong and as rapid an effect as injecting it intravenously, directly into the veins, which is referred to by the addict as "mainlining." This is the most common method of use. As one addict told the author, "Man, there's only one way to take H [heroin]—mainlining—cause that stuff's too expensive to waste."

An addict who "mainlines" usually has a kit of paraphernalia consisting of a hypodermic needle, a medicine dropper or syringe, a bottle cap or spoon, and matches. The powder is mixed with water in the bottle cap or spoon and heated. Once a solution is formed, it is injected intravenously.

The slang terms for heroin are "H," "smack," "horse," "snow," "sugar," "white stuff," and "junk."

Morphine, an odorless white or light brown crystal powder, is available on the market through prescription in tablet and capsule form since it is still used today as a pain reliever. It can be taken orally or injected. Addicts use it, for the most part, only when heroin is unavailable. A number of slang terms used for it are "M," "hard stuff," "white stuff," "Miss Emma," "Unkie," and "morphie."

Codeine, which can be contained in cough syrup or available in tablet and crystal form, is an opium derivative. It is far weaker than the other narcotics. It is taken orally and because of its lack of potency as a narcotic is used only as a supplement to a stronger drug by most addicts. It is also used sometimes to maintain a user until he can obtain heroin or morphine.

For the sake of brevity, the two synthetic opiates meperidine and methadone will not be discussed here (though the methadone maintenance program will be briefly touched upon later in the chapter). Therefore, for information on these drugs the reader is referred to the selected bibliography.

DEPRESSANTS

Depressants are drugs which induce sleep by affecting the CNS. In addition, they are able to reduce tension and anxiety in the individual. And so, depressants act to tranquillize or sedate the person using them. When taken in large quantities over an extended period of time they can be physically addicting like narcotics. An individual can develop a tolerance to their effect and have withdrawal symptoms if use is discontinued after several weeks. Withdrawal symptoms may include nausea, vomiting, running nose, watery eyes, and muscle cramps. Signs like this indicate that the body is reacting to the removal of the drug which it has become dependent upon after prolonged use.

Depressants as a drug category include numerous types of tranquilizers and sedatives. *Barbiturates* are the most widely used of them all. A barbiturate is a sedative and hypnotic. It is commonly seen in various tablet and capsule forms. Overdoses of barbiturates result when they are taken in combination with alcohol or in extreme amounts. If medical treatment is lacking when this occurs, an overdose of this type can result in death.

Barbiturates can be taken a number of ways: orally, rectally, or intravenously. The slang terms for barbiturates are usually associated with the shape or color of the tablet or capsule. Some of these are "barbs," "goofballs," "candy," "reds," "yellows," "reds and blues," "bluebirds," and "blue devils."

STIMULANTS

A stimulant is a drug which acts upon the CNS to reduce hunger, increase alertness, and induce euphoria. This category of drugs includes caffeine (a very weak stimulant), amphetamines, dextro-amphetamine, and metamphetamine. (This is only a partial list.) For the sake of brevity, this section will treat only the most widely used stimulants, that is, amphetamines and cocaine.

Amphetamines do not cause physical dependence. However, even though they are not addicting, they are still able to cause the user to become psychologically dependent on them. (The difference between physically addicted to and psychologically dependent on will be discussed later in the chapter.) Amphetamines have numerous slang names due to the fact that they are available in many different strengths from a number of pharmaceutical concerns and are marketed in various shapes, sizes, and colors. A selection of these terms includes "pep pills," "wake-ups," "truck drivers," "bennies," "eye openers," "greenies," "oranges," "beaches," "bottles," and "dexies."

Cocaine, though a stimulant, is legally classified as a narcotic. This odorless white powder looks something like snow. Cocaine is taken intravenously or sniffed. Some addicts use cocaine in combination with morphine or heroin. When used with heroin it is called "speedball" by the drug abuser. Slang terms for cocaine itself are "coke," "happy dust," "C," and "snow."

HALLUCINOGENS

Hallucinogens are drugs which can induce changes in perception, sensation, emotion, and thinking. Drugs which could be included under this category are LSD, mescaline, psilocybin, DMT, and STP. (Marijuana and some seeds and spices can also produce hallucinogenic effects, though they are chemically distant from the drugs listed above.)

LSD (*d*-lysergic acid diethylamide tartrate 25) is a powerful synthetic chemical. One ounce is enough to provide 300,000 of the usual doses. Currently it is thought that LSD may cause chromosomal damage resulting in congenital birth defects. LSD commonly appears as a white powder or tablet and also as a clear, colorless, odorless liquid. It is impossible to identify visually, and its presence can only be substantiated by qualitative and quantitative analysis tests. LSD is generally taken by mouth. Practically any substance, such as tablet, sugar cube, cookie, or piece of candy can be used. In addition to its abbreviation of LSD is it also referred to in slang terms as: "acid," "sugar," "the Big D," "the cube," and "25."

Mescaline is obtained from the peyote cactus. Hallucinogenic effects of a full dosage may last up to twelve hours. It is dark brown in color and often put into gelatin capsules. It is primarily taken orally. Slang terms for mescaline are: "peyote," "buttons," and "plants."

Psilocybin is extracted from a Mexican mushroom. A dose of 20 to 60 milligrams will give hallucinogenic effects which last up to six hours. Its effects are indistinguishable from those of LSD and mescaline.

DMT (*N,N*-dimethyltryptamine) produces effects similar to LSD but of shorter duration. With DMT the "high" lasts from one to three hours, depending upon the dose. It appears as an orange liquid. Methods of use include intravenous and intramuscular injection. In addition, it can be used to soak marijuana, which is subsequently smoked. DMT is also known to users as the "businessman's special" and the "lunch-hour trip."

STP (4-methyl-2,5-dimethoxy-*a*-methylphenethylamine) is chemically related to mescaline and amphetamine. Its hallucinogenic effects can last three to four days. It is commonly found in tablet or capsule form and taken by mouth. Users often refer to it by the name "serenity" or the phrase "tranquility and peace."

Marijuana, although still regulated by law as a narcotic, is a hallucinogen possessing the elements of both a stimulant and a depressant. It usually looks like green tobacco and often contains seeds and stems. Because of its coarseness, cigarettes are made with a heavy grade of tobacco paper. These cigarettes, or "joints," are usually hand-rolled and closed on both ends because of the loose fill and dryness of the weed. When burning, marijuana has a distinctive odor similar to burning rope or alfalfa. The odor will hang in the air and for a short time is noticeable on the user's breath and clothing. Its major method of use is through smoking, but it can also be taken orally when mixed with tea or bakery goods. The user will attempt to keep the smoke in his lungs as long as possible and will even try to inhale the smoke he has just exhaled. After smoking the joint down as far as possible, he saves the remaining part, called a "roach," and uses it to make new cigarettes. The effects of marijuana are similar to those of alcohol. The total effect of a marijuana "trip" can last from three to five hours. Aftereffects of marijuana are visually minimal. Physical addiction is absent as well, but use of marijuana may result in psychological dependence.

Morning-glory seeds and spices such as *nutmeg* are also being currently used for their ability to produce a hallucinogenic effect. The nonhallucinogenic morning-glory seed is round and can be distinguished from the triangular-shaped one, which can produce hallucinogenic effects.

VOLATILE SUBSTANCES

Many volatile substances can produce a state of intoxication in the individual who inhales them. These liquids can be divided into three groups: *solvents*, *aerosols*, and *anesthetics*. The *solvents* and *anesthetics* are usually poured on a rag and the fumes inhaled, whereas aerosols are directly inhaled by the user from the can. The effects for the user can vary greatly. Stupor, hallucinations, drunkenness, and disorientation are some of the possible reactions.

ILLNESS AND DEATH: BY-PRODUCTS OF DRUG ABUSE

Some attention will now be given to the many physical problems which develop for the drug user. As one would expect, the physical effects vary, according to the type of drug and the amount used: from mild physical ills to death, the range of medical problems possible is quite large. Therefore, each drug category will be treated separately.

Narcotics, the most serious group of drugs subject to abuse, are most widely known for their physically addicting properties and their ability to cause death through overdose (OD). An OD occurs when the injection or "fix" that an addict takes is pure heroin or has a much higher concentration of the narcotic than the addict is accustomed to take. When this happens, the individual becomes comatose. If other addicts are with him when this occurs, they slap him in an effort to wake him then get the individual on his feet and attempt to get him to walk it off. (Surprising as it might seem, this technique is quite effective.) If no one is present when he takes an OD and his lungs become congested, unconsciousness and death may follow. Serum hepatitis or death can also be an end result when an addict injects contaminated material or shares unsterile needles.

Illness is also rampant in a population of narcotic users. An addict's resistance is usually low because most of his money is spent on drugs while he neglects basic necessities. Moreover, since the drug depresses certain sections of the brain, his hunger and thirst drives are reduced. As a result, being habitually malnourished, he is particularly susceptible to tuberculosis and pneumonia. Another hazard is venereal disease, highly prevalent among those who share this lifestyle.

His appearance is also disturbing. If he sniffs heroin, it inflames his nasal and mucous membranes. And if he "mainlines" it repeatedly, the injections cause darkening and hardening of his veins as well as scarred skin at the areas of injection.

As mentioned previously in the chapter, depressants can cause death if taken in excessive amounts or in combination with alcohol. Convulsions are also possible during the period of withdrawal. During this period the drug user frequently has cramps and nausea, and he is agitated and restless. In addition, he may hallucinate and be quite disoriented and confused.

Abusers of stimulants physically deteriorate, losing their desire for food and sleep. They are susceptible to infection, and it is reported that liver and brain damage can result from large doses of a stimulant.

Volatile substances such as solvents are an obvious source of medical problems. Damage to the nervous system, blood, kidneys, and heart can result from certain ingredients in particular types of solvents. Carbon tetrachloride, for example, can cause irreversible kidney and liver damage. Gasoline and naphtha in high concentrations can cause serious heart complications. Furthermore, the lead in gasoline can cause lead poisoning, and aerosols have in a number of cases caused death by freezing the larynx and causing it to contract, or by inducing cardiac arrest.

Drug abuse can, and often does, lead to medical problems which can bring on severe illness and sometimes death.

DRUGS AND MENTAL INSTABILITY

After seeing the physical problems caused by drugs, it is logical to assume that the drug user is also prey to psychological impairment, especially if he was impulsive, immature, non-goal-directed, and self-centered prior to starting on drugs. The first type of user to be discussed in this section is one who is on narcotics, particularly heroin.

When they first start to use this type of drug, narcotic users experience a "high" in which they feel a reduction of tension, relief from worry, and an absence of fear. The drug affects the individual's perception of his troubles; it takes them off his shoulders. However, after a point his body's tissue cells adjust to the presence of the drug. In other words, his body becomes tolerant to the drug, and the result is that he no longer becomes high unless he increases his dosage. After a period of time he will reach the stage where he seeks the drug not so much to achieve a high as to prevent him from going into withdrawal symptoms. It is at this time that the greatest psychological harm is done to the individual. He will go to any extent to maintain his habit. Stealing from his family, "renting" his wife, and cheating his friends can be a way of life for him if he needs funds to support his habit. The emotional stability of the narcotic addict, in particular, is deeply hurt by his drug-centered life.

The individual who uses depressants (sedatives and tranquillizers) is often the person who is upset, anxious, and tense and can't sleep. Those who are in their middle age are particularly susceptible to increased and familiar contact with this type of drug. Sedatives are seen by many adults as a harmless way of unwinding so they can relax and sleep. Unfortunately many adults become used to depressants as an efficient means of helping them counteract their emotional tenseness. The result is that instead of seeking to regulate the amount of work they do or to unwind themselves, they turn more and more to the "magic pill" to do it for them.

Those who are "hooked" (physically addicted to the use of depressants) can have psychological problems similar to those facing narcotic users. The adult user who is not yet addicted to sedatives but takes them in order to deal with anxiety or insomnia should not have mental problems as great as the addict's, but he will still have mental difficulties. Psychologically the individual will be less independent and more vulnerable to tense situations. This occurs to a degree because he has ceased working through his problems and has turned to a drug to do the job instead. In other words, he is seeking to escape from life via, and into, a drug existence.

Persons who abuse stimulants include, for example, the truck driver who takes them to keep awake; the obese individual who has received an indiscriminate diet pill prescription; and the unstable person who is seeking help for his problems and believes his answer lies in the use of a stimulant. The person in the third category is unable to get "high on life" through the natural channels and thus feels he must seek the high which drugs can give him. The inadequate and depressed individual would particularly fall into this category. The primary psychological problem present, then, is that the individual may become dependent upon a pill for his enjoyment and may eventually withdraw from life itself. Furthermore, when he comes down from his high, the depression which follows can present him with even greater emotional difficulties.

LSD abuse has been shrouded with mystical properties by the people who use it. However, there is nothing mysterious or veiled about the dangers present in using it—LSD is capable of doing very great harm. Its psychological effects vary greatly in accordance with the type of person who takes it, the circumstances under which it is taken, and the amount used. During the time that a person is experiencing the effects of the drug (while he is on a "trip"), illusions and hallucinations can occur. The user can have a "good" trip or a "bad" trip. If the trip is bad, the individual can be gripped with terror or horror. For example, he may forget that he is on a drug and fear that he is losing his mind. He sometimes has delusions in which he feels he is invulnerable and attempts to fly or walk in front of a moving vehicle. To further complicate matters, the individual can experience "flashbacks" days, weeks, or even months after his last dose. During a flashback the user enters the LSD-induced state all over again. These experiences, as well as having a bad trip, could cause the individual to become psychotic. And so, instead of having his mind expanded, the user's reward for taking LSD may be to end up in a mental institution—or dead.

"DRUG DEPENDENCE"

Confusion often results when the terms *addiction* and *habituation* are used. They were often used as synonyms, and thus a mix-up resulted as to which drugs cause physical dependence and which drugs cause psychological dependence. The World Health Organization (WHO) has sought to correct this and has introduced a more general term embracing both previous terms—"drug dependence." Drug dependence, according to WHO, is "a state arising from repeated administration of a drug on a periodic or continuous basis." Their new definition is good not only because it eliminates confusion, but also because it forwards the accurate belief that a drug which is *not* physically addicting can still be dangerous.

Formerly, if a drug wasn't capable of causing physical dependence (such as narcotics and depressants), it was not considered dangerous by many users and potential users. They felt that they could use stimulants, hallucinogens, and volatile substances since there would be no withdrawal phase if they stopped using them. However, the absence of a withdrawal phase does not mean that the drug will not lead to psychological dependence.

In other words, the user of a hallucinogen might not suffer any ill effects if he tried to stop using it, but he would feel uncomfortable psychologically and emotionally and subsequently would go back to the drug. Thus a drug which is not physically addicting may produce psychological dependence pressuring the user to continue on drugs; as a result it may be quite dangerous to him, because he can't stop taking it no matter what he says.

DRUGS AND CRIME

The previous sections were presented so that the reader could become somewhat familiar with drugs and the drug problem. The next section will discuss how to identify the drug user. This area is especially important for those in law enforcement because of the relationship between drug abuse and the increase in crime in the nation.

Though some studies have shown that a number of drug users have had trouble with the law before getting involved in the use of drugs, it is also a fact that once they became addicted their crimes became greater and were perpetrated more often. The reason for this is obvious—the high cost of a day's supply of heroin. In addition, the amount of heroin needed increases as time goes by; though the cost of a day's supply may have been $25 in the early stages of an individual's period of addiction, it may jump to over $100 as the addict's tolerance to the drug increases.

Crimes such as theft, prostitution, pushing drugs, and pimping are the most common methods used by addicts to obtain the money they need. However, when their need turns into desperation due to withdrawal symptoms, they may well resort to violence. To avoid going through "cold turkey" withdrawal, nothing will stand in their way—neither family nor friends.

Narcotics are not the only drugs which are a contributing cause of crime. Even volatile substances play a role. It has been documented that impulsive, destructive behavior may be an outcome of solvent-fume inhalation. Though it is admittedly a minor source of crime, it should give the reader an indication of how widespread an effect drugs can have on the crime rate.

IDENTIFYING THE DRUG USER

A chronic drug user will usually do everything possible to conceal his habit.[1] So it is essential for the law enforcement officer to recognize the outward signs and symptoms of drug misuse. One should be alert

[1] Ironically some serious drug abusers openly defy the law. The reasons for this (guilt, defiance, inadequate self-image, deep-seated desire to get caught and to be treated, for example) cannot be discussed here in depth.

to these symptoms, but it is important to realize that *the drug problem is so complex that even experts sometimes have difficulty making accurate diagnoses.* With this in mind, general indications and specific symptoms which point to possible drug abuse will be listed.

Seven general signs which indicate possible drug abuse are:

1. A dramatic decrease in efficiency on the job
2. A deterioration of physical appearance
3. Wearing sunglasses at inappropriate times (indoors)
4. Poor attendance at school or work
5. Wearing long-sleeved shirts all the time
6. Disappearance of small items around the house or at place of work
7. Association with known or suspected drug users

The above may be considered as general indicators to watch for in identifying a possible drug abuser. Some specific characteristics of possible abuse of the following types of drugs will now be presented: narcotics, depressants, stimulants, hallucinogens, and marijuana. Signs of addiction to glue sniffing are also noted.

Due to the severity of his problem the narcotic addict shows certain obvious signs. Here are seven of them:

1. The pupils of his eyes are constricted and fixed.
2. There are "tracks" (scars) on his arms and the backs of his hands.
3. When he is late in getting a "fix" (shot) of heroin, his eyes may be watery and red and his nose dripping, and he may have a nagging cough.
4. He often scratches himself.
5. He is drowsy and lethargic and may sit and nod as if he were trying to stay awake, but he is too tired to accomplish it.
6. During withdrawal he may vomit, have flushed skin, yawn frequently, and twitch.
7. He has a loss of appetite yet is drawn to sweets.

The person who uses depressants excessively will show the symptoms normally associated with alcohol intoxication, without the odor of alcohol on his breath. In addition, the following six characteristics can often be noted:

1. Pupils are dilated.
2. Speech is slurred.
3. He appears to be drowsy.
4. He seems disoriented.

5. He stumbles and staggers when he tries to walk.
6. He has difficulty concentrating.

The stimulant abuser also has dilated pupils. The other signs which point to excessive use of stimulants are:

1. The person appears quite excited, talkative, and active.
2. He may become irritable, argumentative, or upset.
3. He may go for extended periods of time without sleeping or eating.

The behavior of an LSD user, as opposed to the above patterns, may vary greatly in its manifestation. He may be reserved, yet on the other hand he may become terrified and, therefore, very active. Other signs are:

1. Dilation of the pupils
2. Rapid heart rate, increased blood pressure, and an elevated blood sugar level
3. Nausea, chills, flushes, irregular breathing, sweating, and trembling of the hands
4. Possible changes in his sense of sight, hearing, touch, smell, and time

The marijuana user is hard to detect, since he may be able to work under the influence of the drug and with excessive use may appear to be drunk. On the other hand, the individual who has been sniffing glue exhibits several possible symptoms:

1. Odor of the substance he was inhaling on his breath and on his clothing
2. Watery eyes and nose
3. Staggering, drowsiness, or unconsciousness
4. Slurred speech
5. Bad breath

This section has listed information at a fast pace. The reader is not expected to memorize the signs at one sitting. It takes time and practical experience with drug abusers before confidence in this area is attained. Once again it cannot be overemphasized that it is very difficult to recognize some types of drug users. Even experts make mistakes and are unsure in some instances. As a result, the lists presented are not designed to give the reader infallible guides; rather they were provided as a helpful aid in a good number of cases where

there is confusion because of a lack of familiarity with the problem
of drug abuse.

REACTION OF A DRUG ABUSER
TO AN ARRESTING OFFICER

Unpredictable is the term which best describes a user when being
confronted by an arresting officer. How the individual will react is
based to a great extent upon two factors:

1. Whether he is under the influence of a drug or is just in possession of it
2. The type of drug he has taken and the effect it is having on him

When approached by an officer the user can react in several ways.
He can fight, run, give up, or even ignore the situation entirely. If he
takes the first choice, aggression, he may employ any available object
in an effort to surprise and overpower the officer. Included in this
category of weapons are those sharp, hard objects which are on
hand—such as a spoon, needle, or belt. This type of hostility is often
attempted by the user who is in possession of a drug but has not yet
taken it and by the person whose faculties have not been significantly impaired by the drug he has taken.

As might be expected, there is also a danger that the user will try
to run to avoid arrest. If he sees an opportunity to escape, his fear of
being locked up will naturally induce the person to attempt it. Since
the euphoric effect of certain drugs may also aid an individual to
withstand the pain of prolonged exertion, chasing such a user might
be quite difficult. Therefore, ensuring that all avenues of escape are
adequately covered must be a routine precaution.

For the majority of drug users, however, giving up, claiming
innocence, or even ignoring the situation seem to be the most
reasonable modes of action when confronted by an officer. Usually,
then, firmly and clearly indicating to a suspect that he is being placed
under arrest should be sufficient.

Yet the officer must still be aware of the other possible reactions,
for his safety is always threatened by the unpredictability of the drug
abuser population he is dealing with. It is for this reason that the
officer has been introduced to the other less frequently encountered
reaction patterns.

TREATMENT FOR THE DRUG ABUSER

Treatment centers for the drug abuser are being opened throughout
the country. Private and governmental agencies are searching for and

experimenting with numerous approaches to aid the drug user so he can break the bonds of addiction and dependence. However, to this point no short-term treatment program has been found which has been overwhelmingly successful with large groups of addicts. Yet there have been approaches which have had "good" success rates with limited numbers through the utilization of an extensive program.

Presently there are three primary approaches to the drug problem, though there are many versions of each type. One method is a *group therapy program*, the kind run by Synanon. It is privately run, deals with small numbers, is generally staffed by former users, and to date has had an impressive success rate.

The second major approach is *civil commitment*. Both California and New York are utilizing this type of program. Here the arrested user can choose to stand trial or enter a rehabilitation program lasting about three years. If the addict does not choose to enter the program and is found guilty while standing trial, the authorities in California and New York will probably send him to the rehabilitation-oriented program despite his original objection.

The third technique is the *methadone maintenance program.* In this program the addict is given methadone as a substitute for heroin. As well as receiving methadone, the addict takes part in a program including schooling, therapy, and work. It must be realized that the methadone program would probably be less effective if it were used alone.

However, though these programs are the most ambitious and comprehensive ever attempted, as was noted previously, they still have not been able to claim a high cure rate. If this is so, what is the answer? Dr. Donald Louria may have touched upon a possible reason when he wrote recently in *The New York Times* that none of these programs deals with the real problem. Heroin abuse is a symptom; poverty, undereducation, inadequate housing, prejudice, and a lack of job opportunities are the underlying culprits.

WHAT WAS COVERED IN THIS CHAPTER

In accordance with what Dr. Louria said above and with what most narcotics officials have expressed recently, education seems to be one of the most effective means of attacking the drug problem. If factual information is made available, the young will realize what drugs really hold for them. If children are not given the impression that life is unbearable without drugs or alcohol, they will not seek them.

It is the job of parents to know about drugs in order to teach their children and answer their questions intelligently. Moreover, it is the responsibility of those in law enforcement to understand the problem well enough to talk about it to an individual or a group without wondering whether the facts presented are accurate.

This chapter was designed to give the reader an introduction to drug addiction, drug abuse, the problems of the drug addict, signs of drug abuse, and other pertinent areas touching on this problem. In addition, on the next two pages is a chart which summarizes a number of the points which are too lengthy to be summarized here. This chapter should be read and reread, and at least some of the material listed in the Selected Bibliography on the drug problem at

Properties of Various Drugs*

Drugs	Pharmocologic Classification	Bureau of Narcotics and Dangerous Drugs Controls	Medical Use	Potential for Physical Dependence
Morphine (an opium derivative)	Central Nervous System Depressant	Narcotic Schedule II Controlled Substances Act of 1970 (C.S.A.)	To relieve pain	Yes
Heroin (a morphine derivative)	Depressant	Narcotic Schedule I C.S.A.	To relieve pain	Yes
Codeine (an opium derivative	Depressant	Narcotic Schedule II C.S.A.	To relieve pain and coughing	Yes
Paregoric (preparation containing opium)	Depressant	Narcotic Schedule III C.S.A.	For sedation and to counteract diarrhea	Yes
Meperidine (synthetic morphine-like drug)	Depressant	Narcotic Schedule II C.S.A.	To relieve pain	Yes
Methadone (synthetic morphine-like drug)	Depressant	Narcotic Schedule II C.S.A.	To relieve pain	Yes
Cocaine	Central Nervous System Stimulant	Stimulant Schedule II C.S.A.	Local anesthetic	No
Marihuana	Hallucinogen	Hallucinogen Schedule I (Per Marihuana Tax Act, 1937, plus subsequent restrictive legislation which covered marihuana and narcotics together) C.S.A.	None	No
Barbiturates (e.g., amobarbital, pentobarbital, secobarbital)	Depressant	Depressant Schedules III & IV C.S.A.	For sedation, sleep-producing, epilepsy, high blood pressure	Yes
Amphetamine drugs (e.g., amphetamine, dextroam-phetamine, methampheta-mine—also known as desoxyephedrine)	Stimulant	Stimulant Schedule II C.S.A.	For mild depression, anti-appetite, narcolepsy	No
LSD (also mescaline, peyote, psilocybin, DMT, STP, THC)	Hallucinogen	Hallucinogen Schedule I C.S.A.	(Medical research only)	No
Glue (also paint thinner, lighter fluid)	Depressant	No Federal controls. Glue sales restricted in some states.	None	Unknown

*Reprinted courtesy of Smith, Kline and French Laboratories the end of this chapter should be studied. The reader must become well informed about drugs. If the law enforcement officer is not familiar with drugs and the problems they cause, what can be expected of the other citizens of this nation?

REVIEW

1. What is a narcotic?
2. What are the three main types of drugs classified as narcotics?
3. What are the three ways in which heroin can be taken?
4. What are the items in an addict's kit?

Potential for Psychological Dependence	Tolerance	Possible Effects When Abused	How Taken When Abused	Penalties
Yes	Yes	Drowsiness or stupor, pinpoint pupils	Orally or by injection	Penalties for simple possession Unlawful possession of any controlled substance: a. First offense—not more than 1 year's imprisonment and/or a fine of not more than $5,000.
Yes	Yes	Same as morphine	Sniffed or by injection	
Yes	Yes	Drowsiness, pinpoint pupils	Orally (usually as cough syrup)	b. Second offense—not more than 2 years' imprisonment and/or a fine of not more than $10,000.
Yes	Yes	Same as morphine	Orally or by injection	Special first offender provision for simple possession
Yes	Yes	Similar to morphine, except that at higher doses, excitation, tremors and convulsions occur	Orally or by injection	In dealing with a person who has not been convicted of any previous violations of this Act or of any other U.S. law related to narcotics, marihuana, depressant or stimulant drugs, the Court has the following option: It may, after trial of the accused or his plea of guilty, place him on 1 year or less probation without entering a judgment of guilty. Upon satisfactory completion of that probation, the Court may dismiss the proceeding against the person. A private record of the proceeding is retained by the Department of Justice solely for the purpose of preventing the offender from qualifying for this provision in any subsequent proceeding.
Yes	Yes	Same as morphine	Orally or by injection	
Yes	No	Extreme excitation, tremors, hallucinations	Sniffed or by injection	
Yes	No	Drowsiness or excitability, talkativeness, laughter, hallucinations	Smoked or orally	
Yes	Yes	Drowsiness, staggering, slurred speech	Orally or by injection	NOTE: Preparations containing specified minimal amounts of codeine and paregoric are classified in Schedule V by Federal regulations. These preparations may be sold without a prescription only by a pharmacist and only if the person is at least 18 years of age.
Yes	Yes	Excitation, dilated pupils, tremors, talkativeness, hallucinations	Orally or by injection	
Yes	Yes	Excitation, hallucinations, rambling speech	Orally or by injection	
Yes	Yes	Staggering, drowsiness slurred speech, stupor	Inhaled	Freely available as commercial products, except that some states have laws forbidding the sale of glue to persons under 18.

5. What is a depressant?
6. What is a barbiturate?
7. What are the slang terms for barbiturates given in this chapter?
8. What is a stimulant?
9. What are hallucinogens?
10. What is a "joint"? A "roach"?
11. What are some of the physical effects of drug abuse?
12. Does drug abuse have a relationship with mental instability? If so, how?
13. What is the World Health Organization's definition of "drug dependence"?
14. What are seven general signs which indicate possible drug abuse?
15. What three treatment approaches are available to drug users today?

SELECTED BIBLIOGRAPHY ON THE DRUG PROBLEM

Books

Barber, B.: *Drugs and Society*, Russell Sage Foundation, New York, 1967. 212 pp.

Bejerot, N.: *Addiction and Society*, Charles C Thomas, Springfield, Ill., 1970. 320 pp.

Bennett, J. C., and G. D. Demos: *Drug Abuse and What We Can Do about It*, Charles C Thomas, Springfield, Ill., 1970. 136 pp.

Blum, R. H., and Associates: *The Utopias: The Use and Users of LSD-25*, Atherton, New York, 1964. 304 pp.

Blumer, H.: *The World of Youthful Drug Use*, School of Criminology, University of California, Berkeley, 1967. 85 pp.

Cohen, S.: *The Drug Dilemma*, McGraw-Hill, New York, 1969. 174 pp.

DeQuincey, T.: *Confessions of an English Opium Eater*, Dent, London, 1967. 272 pp.

Eldridge, E.: *Narcotics and the Law*, (2d ed.), University of Chicago Press, 1967. 246 pp.

Harney, M. L., and J. C. Cross: *The Narcotic Officer's Notebook*, Charles C Thomas, Springfield, Ill., 1961. 251 pp.

Harris, John D.: *The Junkie Priest: Father Daniel Egan, S.A.*, Coward-McCann, New York, 1964. 254 pp.

Hoffer, A., and H. Osmond: *The Hallucinogens*, Academic Press, New York, 1967. 626 pp.

Larner, Jeremy (ed.): *The Addict in the Street*, Grove Press, New York, 1964. 288 pp.

Laurie, P.: *Drugs: Medical, Psychological and Social Factors*, Penguin, Baltimore, 1969. 174 pp.

Louria, D. B.: *The Drug Scene*, McGraw-Hill, New York, 1968. 215 pp.

Polsky, N.: *Hustlers, Beats and Others*, Aldine, Chicago, 1967. 368 pp.

Schmidt, Jacob Edward: *Narcotic Lingo and Lore*, Charles C Thomas, Springfield, Ill., 1959. 199 pp.

Yablonsky, L.: *The Tunnel Back: Synanon*, Macmillan, New York, 1965. 403 pp.

Pamphlets

Bureau of Narcotics and Dangerous Drugs: *Public Speaking on Drug Abuse Prevention: A Handbook for the Law Enforcement Officer*, U.S. Government Printing Office, 1970. 40 pp.

Drug Abuse: A Manual for Law Enforcement Officers, 5th ed., Smith, Kline and French Laboratories, Philadelphia, 1968. 68 pp.

National Clearinghouse for Drug Abuse Information: *A Federal Source Book: Answers to the Most Frequently Asked Questions about Drug Abuse*, U.S. Government Printing Office, 1970. 30 pp.

National Institute of Mental Health: *LSD: Some Questions and Answers*, rev. ed., U.S. Government Printing Office, 1970. 10 pp.

National Institute of Mental Health: *Narcotics: Some Questions and Answers*, rev. ed., U.S. Government Printing Office, 1970. 8 pp.

National Institute of Mental Health: *Sedatives: Some Questions and Answers*, rev. ed., U.S. Government Printing Office, 1970. 8 pp.

National Institute of Mental Health: *Stimulants: Some Questions and Answers*, U.S. Government Printing Office, 1970. 10 pp.

National Institute of Mental Health: *Volatile Substances: Some Questions and Answers*, U.S. Government Printing Office, 1968. 8 pp.

Office of Juvenile Delinquency and Youth Development, Social and Rehabilitation Service—Brothman, R., and Suffett, F.: *Youthful Drug Use*, U.S. Government Printing Office, 1970. 39 pp.

Articles

Anslinger, Harry J.: "Narcotics Addiction as Seen by the Law-Enforcement Officer," *Federal Probation*, vol. 21, pp. 34—41, June 1957.

Black, J.: "The 'Speed' That Kills—or Worse," *New York Times Magazine*, June 21, 1970, p. 14.

Eddy, N. B.: "The History of the Development of Narcotics," *Law and Contemporary Problems*, vol. 22, no. 1, pp. 3—8, 1957.

Hills, S. L.: "Marijuana, Morality and the Law," *Crime and Delinquency*, January 1970, pp. 57—66.

Macmillan, W. L., Jr.: "The Scent of Danger," *The Police Chief*, vol. 20, no. 5, pp. 42–44, 1963.

Pet, D. D., and J. C. Ball: "Marijuana Smoking in the United States," *Federal Probation*, vol. 32, no. 3, pp. 8–15, 1968.

section three

Interviewing and Interrogation

chapter nine

Principles
in Interviewing

Law enforcement agents are constantly involved in the physical pursuit of lawbreakers. Newspapers, TV, and magazines deluge millions of citizens daily with pictures of peace officers cornering suspects and bringing them to justice. Yet catching a supposed violater of the law is only part of the task.

After an individual is apprehended, the long hard period of questioning must begin. If the individual does not confess to the crime and evidence is lacking, further investigation must be carried out to find would-be witnesses or new suspects. Because of the nature of their work, officers are faced daily with the job of interviewing.

In addition to interviewing suspects and witnesses, the officer is often required to hold formal and informal sessions with youths on probation, citizens filing complaints, and even their own subordinates in the department who may be having some difficulties on the job. Because of his constant involvement in the interviewing process, today's officer obviously is expected to be able to function adequately as an interviewer. This chapter is designed to assist the reader in developing his interviewing ability by introducing him to some basic principles of this technique. With this as a goal, the first obvious step will be to discuss what an interview basically is.

WHAT IS AN INTERVIEW?

An interview is primarily a process in which one gathers information. In other words, it is a form of communication, like conversation, but it has a definite aim. The goal of an interview can take many forms—for example, to determine with whom a teenager spends his time, or what happened on a particular day, or where a particular suspect was at a certain time.

A law enforcement officer is constantly involved in purposeful communications with people. It's part of his daily activity. The way he conducts these interviews, both formal and informal, determines how successful he is in making the progress he desires. Consequently, the officer should be well versed in several basic interviewing principles.

THE INTERVIEW RELATIONSHIP

Productive interviews are based on the formation of a special relationship between the interviewer and the interviewee. This relationship may vary according to the type of interview, but whatever the purpose of the interaction is, the interviewer should lay the groundwork as soon as possible. Before seeing the person to be interviewed, the interviewer must decide the type of picture he wants to present.

For example, the interviewer may feel that a parolee must be allowed to voluntarily open up to him even though he is already familiar with the parolee's present problem. If the interviewer greeted the parolee with a statement such as, "You're here because you're in some sort of trouble, aren't you?" the parolee would probably assume that the interviewer had already prejudged his situation. An alternate approach might be to simply say, "How are you, John? What did you want to see me about?" In this way, the interviewer is not indicating that the parolee is being judged on his past actions. The parolee can also reasonably assume that the interviewer is willing to listen.

In a situation where an officer is interviewing a subordinate, the interviewer may feel that it is important to display open-mindedness and a willingness to assist the subordinate in working out his problem. If he is being charged with brutality or negligence, for example, the superior officer should indicate an awareness of the seriousness or implications involved in the situation. This information would indicate to the subordinate that the interviewer was willing to use an honest approach by revealing what he had already heard concerning the situation.

In addition, the interviewer should firmly establish the fact that he is prepared to extend full support to the accused if he is innocent of the charges brought against him. This should reassure the subordinate that he is being interviewed by a person who is firm, fair, and interested in his welfare. By giving the interviewee this impression at the outset, the rest of the interaction will prove more fruitful than if he were unaware as to how the interviewer felt about him and the charges pending against him.

In the case of a suspect, the officer might want to give the impression that the suspect had better "level" with him because he is not willing to accept any nonsense. On the other hand, the officer might want to display complete ignorance of the situation so that he can determine whether the suspect will lie if given the opportunity. Whatever approach he chooses, he must present his image at the beginning of the interview because it will affect his relationship with the suspect for the rest of the meeting.

This concept of building a sound interviewee-interviewer relationship in the early part of the interaction cannot be overemphasized. If the officer does not set the stage for what he hopes to accomplish, the whole interview may easily prove to be a failure. In many cases, the interviewee will be especially sensitive to how the officer reacts to him. How the officer tips his hand could cost him more than he can afford. If a youth believes the officer is just going to preach to him and prejudge him like his father always does, the officer may never be able to gain the rapport with him that's needed in delicate situations. So the officer must strive to be aware of what is said and how he says it early in the interview, keeping in mind what picture he wants the suspect to have of him.

PHYSICAL CONDITIONS UNDER WHICH THE INTERVIEW IS CONDUCTED

One of the main factors in the building up of a relationship concerns the physical conditions under which the interview is conducted. Under this heading two things will be discussed:

1. Place to hold the interview
2. Interruptions during the interview

There is no hard and fast description which applies to the type of environment in which the interview should be held. However, some basic hints can be given. First, try to hold interviews in a private area. The interviewee will relate more to the interviewer if he feels that what he says will not be overheard. Second, the makeup of the room should not be distracting. Open files on other persons that were interviewed should not be displayed; the desk, be it cluttered or uncluttered, must not serve as a distraction to the interviewer or the interviewee. Basically the area in which an interview is conducted should be conducive to privacy and should not work against the interviewer by distracting the interviewee.

Interruptions during interviewing can bring to an abrupt halt any progress that is being made. They can also cause the mood of the interview to be destroyed so badly that any future progress is eliminated. Persons who interrupt others during an interview do it because of ignorance. Because they have never been involved in interviewing, they fail to recognize the harm they have done by destroying, in a matter of seconds, the rapport so carefully built up by the interviewer. To remedy this problem, interviewers have taken the time to indoctrinate those around them not to break in during an interview *for any reason whatsoever!*

On the other hand, if interruptions are unavoidable, this problem can still be handled satisfactorily. If the phone rings or someone enters, the interviewer should first turn to whomever he is interviewing and excuse himself for having to interrupt the session. When this happens, he must remember what was being said when the interruption occurred. After the person who broke in has left, the interviewer should briefly excuse himself again, then say something like "Well, you were saying . . ." or "We were discussing . . . ." By this means the interviewee will realize that the interruption did not distract the interviewer's attention from him. This should at least be of assistance in picking up the pieces of the interview as best as possible.

Primarily, the physical surroundings are important in that they can hinder or help the interviewer demonstrate his interest in the interviewee. Conveying interest is an essential tool of the interviewer. Therefore, the physical setting should be manipulated as much as possible so that the interest effect is enhanced.

CONVEYING INTEREST

While a person is being interviewed, he must feel that he has the complete attention of the interviewer. If not, the interviewee will feel neglected and wonder about the sincerity of the interviewer. More can be gained by a few good interviews than by a large number carried out in a half-hearted manner. A detective might be heard saying, "I just don't understand it. Today I saw seven witnesses and didn't get a shred of evidence. Yesterday I saw two people for only twenty minutes, and I wound up with some great leads. I think I just wasn't concentrating on what was happening during the interviews." Therefore, if complete attention isn't given to the subject during an interview, it can prove to be fruitless.

Before the interview starts is the best time to show the individual that he will be given proper consideration because someone is interested in him. This can be accomplished by greeting him properly. If he is not a close friend, he should be received warmly and confidently. To be aloof or show an unrealistic amount of affection would be incorrect. The interviewee should feel that the interviewer is *naturally* interested in talking to him and hearing what he has to say. In trying to make the person feel accepted, the interviewer often makes a poor impression by being overly friendly. He shouldn't portray the desire to have a "buddy-buddy" relationship with the interviewee. This would prove to be a great mistake on the interviewer's part. An interviewee can easily see when he is not being treated honestly and openly.

Another primary method which an officer can use to indicate his interest in the interviewee is to give him the impression that he is not in a hurry to terminate the interview. If the individual feels the interviewer is trying to get rid of him, feelings of hurt, anger, or boredom may be aroused. Three time periods during the interview should be handled in a particular way. These three fall into natural divisions:

1. The beginning of the interview
2. The bulk of the interview
3. The end of the interview

At the beginning of the interview the individual should be given time to move on to the topic he will present. Hurrying him will serve only to alienate and confuse him. Unless the officer is consciously trying to put pressure on the person being interviewed, ample time must be allowed for him to adjust to the situation.

During the interview the officer may often be tempted to interrupt the subject. However, doing this to move the interview along might also demonstrate to the individual that the interviewer is in a rush. In addition, by breaking into what he is saying, the officer often lessens his chances of hearing essential information that the interviewee was working up to before the interruption.

When the session is about to come to a close because the officer has not received the information he wanted or because the time allotted for it has elapsed, the interviewer should not be blunt in ending it. Being curt will damage any rapport that might have been established, as in the case of interviewing a parolee. In the instance where a witness is being questioned, any future help from him might be eliminated if the session is not ended properly.

Therefore, the officer must not give the interviewee the impression that he is in a hurry, whether at the beginning, middle, or end of the session. To do so might move the interview along, but a shorter session that is not productive wastes more time than it saves.

UNDERSTANDING THE INTERVIEWEE

To be able effectively to express interest in the person being interviewed, the interviewer should have as good an understanding of the individual and his circumstances as is possible. Often the interviewer finds it hard to understand the person he is required to interview. Even when this occurs, the officer should still attempt to attain some grasp of what the interviewee is like. In this way, even if the officer cannot completely break down the wall which divides him from, say, a youth on probation, at least by finding out something about the nature of their differences he can possible avoid making the distance between them any greater than necessary.

One particular way to enhance the development of an understanding of an interviewee is to adopt his *internal frame of reference*. This is accomplished by putting oneself in the person's place in an effort to comprehend how he views himself and the situation he is in.

A police officer at the scene of a robbery may find it hard to deal with a reluctant witness. He may feel that the person is a coward and a poor citizen since he doesn't want to get involved and testify. This type of attitude on the part of the officer, whether it is valid or invalid, will only cause him to reject the witness and in turn be rejected himself. Upon seeing the officer's unaccepting reaction, the witness may feel that the officer does not understand his situation. Therefore, the witness will reject anything the officer may say, no matter how logical it may be.

Better results in a situation like this might be achieved if the officer assumed the witness's internal frame of reference. Doing this might help him to better understand why the witness refuses to testify. In the above illustration, if the officer realized that the person might be afraid for his family and himself, this could be a stepping-off point for convincing him to testify. Instead of ridiculing the witness in an attempt to shame him into testifying, which would probably have an opposite effect, the officer might try to build rapport and then persuade the witness. It is often possible to get a person to accept something, which he might ordinarily have rejected, by presenting it after a period of rapport building. The following dialogue illustrates this idea.

Officer: What is your name?

Witness: Why should I give it to you? I'm not going to get involved, no matter what.

Officer: You don't think you should?

Witness: No, I've got enough problems.

Officer: Yes, I think I can see what you mean—being a witness would be an inconvenience.

Witness: Not only that, I'm afraid too.

Officer: Yes, I felt that you were concerned about your safety.

Witness: Why should I put myself out on a limb?

Officer: Things sure are getting bad on the streets, aren't they?

Witness: They sure are.

Officer: I guess that's why I asked you to testify. I realize that it would be an inconvenience and you're concerned about yourself and your family, but we have to stop these criminals from feeling that they can intimidate citizens, or else they're going to take over. No street will be safe, and there will be no end to it.

Witness: Yes, I agree, and I wish I could help you out, but you understand my position.

Officer: Oh, I do, but it's good citizens like you who can work as a team with law enforcement officers to stand up to crime. Standing up to it is the sensible thing to do. You know what happens when you start appeasing criminals. I'll be quite candid with you. I feel I've gotten to know you better, and I'm worried, because if good citizens like you won't help us, what chance do we have to stop the spread of crime?

Witness: You're right, I guess. It is true that the time has come for us to stop crime. Criminals are always getting away with everything.

Officer: They sure are. It's time we stopped them.

Witness: By the way, my name is _____. I guess I can help you after all. . . .

This is how one type of situation can be handled by using the technique of putting oneself in the other fellow's shoes.

The reader should have noticed that throughout the interview the officer *accepted* the witness, rather than rejecting him because of any view he expressed. The officer was permissive and friendly, and the individual didn't feel threatened.

For the most part, the attitude of the interviewer was *nonjudgmental*. He did not agree or disagree with what the witness said; he indicated that he did not condemn him for the way he felt. As a result, the interviewee felt secure enough to continue to express his feelings to the officer. This is desirable in all interviewing sessions. When the officer's interviewing attitude is nonjudgmental, the interviewee is naturally inclined to continue to relate the truth. This will be the case during the first interview and subsequent ones as well.

SILENCE IN THE INTERVIEW SETTING

As well as maintaining a nonjudgmental attitude, the ability of the interviewer to remain silent during an interview is another essential technique which should be practiced. For the inexperienced interviewer this method is one of the hardest to master. This is especially so in today's society, where life is not geared to periods of silence. During a conversation, if one person stops talking, the other feels it's his social duty to keep the interaction moving by saying something. Houses come equipped with TV sets and phones, cars with radios and tape decks—even places of worship provide time during the service for music and oral prayers. Today's society is unaccustomed to silence. Therefore, when a person begins interviewing and is told he must often be silent, it's common for him to become a bit anxious.

After one minute's silence, it may seem to the interviewer that it has been fifteen minutes since anything was said. Yet, despite the unpleasantness of not allowing oneself to say anything, silence on the part of the interviewer is often quite necessary. If the interviewer does not observe this rule, he may miss information which the interviewee would have transmitted to him had he remained silent.

When the interviewee stops talking or refuses to say anything, it can be for a number of reasons. A few of the principal ones are:

1. The interviewee could be thinking about what he's going to say next.
2. He might be embarrassed about what he has just revealed to the interviewer.
3. He could be waiting to find out the reaction of the interviewer to what he has said.

4. The individual might be expressing anger.
5. He might possibly be confused as to what he should say next.

The first reason listed above is often the source of an individual's silence during the interview. Time is often needed by the individual to think through the question he has been asked. If he's not given an opportunity to think, but is interrupted by the interviewer, essential information may never come to light.

A good interviewer will give the person he's interviewing ample time to reply. In a good number of cases a delinquent may not be able to communicate with his elders because they are always bombarding him with questions and never allotting him enough time to consider what is being asked. Rapport is built quickly with youths by the individual who is willing to both listen out their comments and wait out their periods of reflection.

Embarrassment can also be the cause of the interviewee's silence. When a delinquent has admitted to the use of drugs or a pedophiliac has confessed to molesting children, and even in a minor case such as when a subordinate admits that he made a mistake in judgment, silence will often follow what is said due to their embarrassment at what they have revealed to the interviewer.

Another reason for silence on the part of the interviewee is that he is waiting to see the reaction of the interviewer to what he has just said. In this instance, if the interviewer remains composed and shows no expression, a major battle can be won. For example, if a former drug addict notes that he has been tempted to go back to drugs while on parole, he will certainly wait to see if the interviewer says or shows through facial expression that he is worried about him, disappointed in him, etc. If the interviewer can remain calm and silent, the ex-addict will stop looking for a tipoff on how the interviewer feels and delve more deeply into why he was tempted to go back to drugs. In other words, silence in this instance particularly will result in more information being elicited from the interviewee. Moreover, when he fails to observe any particular emotion, the interviewee will not be reluctant to continue because he thinks the interviewer is disgusted or disapproves of what he has done.

Anger is a great block to the flow of communications between an interviewer and an interviewee. It is also a mask, in some cases, for anxiety. When a person is angry, he will object to communicating anything to the individual he is angry with. In addition, if the interviewer has touched upon a sore point, causing the person to feel anxious, the latter will often cover up by displaying anger. These forms of anger can be manifested by means of silence. Defiant silence is a common way for immature individuals to show their anger. Therefore, it is one of the primary reasons for silence in the interview situation.

The final reason for silence listed above was confusion. In this instance, the interviewee is puzzled as to what the interviewer wants him to say. Once again silence can pay off if the interviewer is able to keep quiet. This can be illustrated by the following conversation.

> Officer: Good morning, ma'am. I'm from the 113th Precinct, and I'm inquiring about Mr. John Doe.
> Landlady: Yes, what did you want to know about him?
> Officer: Tell me whatever you can.
> Landlady: (*Silent pause*) Well, if it's about the people he's been hanging around with. . . .

In the above few lines one can see that the officer did not commit himself and did not rush the landlady. She was confused about what he wanted to know, but evidently had some idea. The officer had a few specific questions, but he knew he could always ask them at the end of the interview. If he had rushed in and broken the silence, he might never have received the information the landlady thought he was looking for. Once again silence paid off.

Silence does indeed benefit the interviewer. As noted earlier, though, it is not easy to remain silent. Yet, if nothing else, a good listener can provide an ideal atmosphere for someone to talk freely. The ability to remain silent can mean the difference between a good interview and a mediocre one.

NONVERBAL COMMUNICATION

Now that we have emphasized the need for an interviewer to remain silent, the question that comes to mind is: What should the interviewer be doing during these silent periods? In addition to considering what he should say next as well as concentrating on why the person is silent, he should be aware of what the interviewee is transmitting to him nonverbally. Nonverbal communication is a process of transmitting information through the use of physical cues without employing any words. It can be effected in any number of ways. Three of them involve the use of voice tone, facial expression, and body gestures.

Voice tone is a common method of nonverbal communication. The way an individual says something is often more pertinent than what he says. If a subordinate said to you in a strained tone that he wasn't upset over the new shift he had been assigned to work, which would give you more information? What he said or how he said it? Naturally, how he said it.

Facial expressions can also give the interviewer much information. For example, if a witness grimaces when the interviewer mentions that he is aware that the witness is acquainted with the primary suspect, one may guess that a sore point has been touched upon. The example is simple, but getting information by observing facial expressions is a basic technique which is often neglected by novice interviewers.

The third type of nonverbal communication technique mentioned above was body gestures. Body gestures refer to the mannerisms of the individual which can give the officer clues as to his state of mind. In other words, if the individual is constantly moving around in his chair or pulling at parts of his face (e.g., earlobes) with his hand, it may indicate that he is nervous and jittery. Once again this is an oversimplification, but the point made is valid. Once the interviewer is able to observe basic types of nonverbal communication, he should be able to develop his talents further in this area.

It should be realized too, of course, that just as the interviewer gets clues from what he observes nonverbally, so does the interviewee, even though he may not have had formal training in this area. If he is talking and the interviewer looks bored, he will hesitate to go on. If the interviewer shows a surprised expression when given some information by a witness, the individual will be alert to the fact that what he said was important. Nonverbal communication is not only something worth studying in order to be aware of what the interviewee is communicating consciously or unconsciously; it also reveals how the officer is responding nonverbally to what is said or done. Being alert to this area can add much to the interviewer's ability.

QUESTIONING THE INTERVIEWEE

Despite the attention previously given to the importance of silence and nonverbal communication, there are times when one must ask questions. Three subtopics will be touched upon in this area. They are:

1. The rules of questioning
2. The difference between closed questions and open-ended questions
3. Leading questions

Questions should always have a clear purpose. This is the basic rule from which all the other rules concerning questioning are derived. Questions are not asked just to satisfy curiosity or to fill lag time in the interview session. Basically they are asked when:

1. Further information is required.
2. The interviewee has not furnished some essential facts.
3. The interviewee is going far off the track.

If questions need to be asked for any or all of the above reasons, they should be *simple*, *indirect*, and *neutral*. If one asks complex questions, the interviewee may become more entangled than before, and the questions may do more harm than good. A direct question can put the person on his guard. Always attempt to use an indirect approach. In addition, try to ensure that the question will not influence his answer but rather elicit what he really feels about the subject. For example, if an officer wanted to know where a person was at a particular time, he could ask directly or indirectly:

"Where were you at 10 P.M. on Tuesday, the 23rd of August?"
or
"No doubt it won't be easy to remember everything that happened back on August 23rd, but would you tell me in as much detail as possible what you did on that day?"

Both the above questions are asking for the same information. Yet the second version tends to be more indirect and neutral. With an indirect question it may take a little longer to get the information, but the information one gets will usually be more reliable—especially when interviewing a suspect who will be on guard as to what he says in reply to questions.

Basically there are two types of questions, closed and open-ended. Closed questions usually elicit only a yes or no answer. They are also more specific and directed at limited areas, whereas an open-ended question is just that, a question which opens the door to varied new information. An example of an open question is as follows:

"Could you tell me a bit more about your next-door neighbor?"
A closed question might be phrased:
"Is your neighbor a hard person to get along with?"
Both types of questions are useful. The open-ended questions would be used, in most cases, in the early part of the interview when not much information is known by the interviewer. He asks general questions to gather general groupings of data. Toward the end of the session closed questions are most often used in order to check on

facts which might have been glossed over when the interviewee commented on the areas he discussed earlier in the interview. So both types of questions are worthwhile. However, the interviewer should be aware that he will normally not receive a lengthy, in-depth answer to the closed type. Furthermore, closed questions, as the reader probably noticed, are quite direct and should therefore be used sparingly.

The final subtopic which shall be dealt with here concerns the use of leading questions. Leading questions, as the term implies, are those questions which give the interviewee an indication of what answer is expected of him. Leading questions can take two forms; below are examples of both forms:

"Anyone who would beat up an old lady is sick, isn't he?"

"Do you think anyone who would beat up an old lady is sick or a coward?"

In the first question the interviewer took only one position. On the other hand, in the second instance the interviewer was trying to lead the interviewee into agreeing with one of two answers.

Both types of leading questions can be used, but the interviewer should be fully aware of their limitations. Leading questions are a very narrow form of the direct question, and they give the interviewee information on how the interviewer feels. And so, if a leading question must be used—when necessary to pin an individual down on some issue, for example—it must be done with a realization that the results could be undesirable if the interviewee does not follow the lead and agree to what is being suggested. Moreover, even if he does agree, it still can be detrimental to the interview process. In the example used above concerning the mugging of an old lady, the interviewee might agree that a person had to be sick to commit such an act, but the results of such an admission might make him afraid to reveal subsequently that he, or a member of his family, committed the crime. Because of the leading question, he knows how the interviewer feels, and he has also expressed how he himself feels. As a result, it has been made very difficult for him to admit any involvement in the crime. To reiterate, then, leading questions should not be used too often, and when they are employed, the interviewer should be fully aware of the chance he is taking by using such a technique.

Having examined the use of questions to some extent, some final comments on the use of questioning are in order. First, use questions with care and only when necessary. Questions usually reveal to the interviewee specific areas that the interviewer is interested in; this should be avoided, because the purpose of the interview is to elicit information from the individual, allowing him to learn as little as possible about the interviewer. In addition, when a question is asked, it often causes an interruption in the person's train of thought, resulting in possible confusion and, inevitably, a loss of continuity in the session. Such breaks in the thread of the interview often result in information being left out by the individual when he returns to what was being discussed prior to the interruption.

Therefore, the interviewer should attempt to ask as few questions as possible. Furthermore, before asking a question, as a check on himself the interviewer should:

1. Ask himself whether the question is really necessary
2. Determine what kind of question he's going to ask—direct or indirect, leading or neutral, closed or open-ended

If all these points are taken into account, the questions used by the interviewer will be few and presented properly under the right circumstances.

With all these factors in mind, only one other point will be made in this section, namely, the procedure to follow when the interviewee asks the interviewer a question. This situation can be handled in the following ways:

1. Parry the question whenever possible.
2. Give short answers which contain no pertinent information.

In other words, if a witness asks the investigator, "Do you think he's guilty?" the investigator might parry, "Why, do you?" In this instance he's reflecting what the witness is interested in knowing while putting the focus on him without answering the question. In the case where a probation officer is meeting a young ex-drug addict who is assigned to him, the young man may ask him how his wife is, seeing a picture of her on the desk. The probation officer does not want to talk about his own life, but to work with the youth on his. Yet, for the probation officer to say "None of your business" or to ignore the well-meant question would harm the rapport which might have been built up between them. Instead, a short answer is better, one having no pertinent information which could be followed up by the youth; an example would be, "She's fine, thank you."

The way in which questions are handled by the interviewer can mean the difference between an interview that functions well and one that turns into just an ordinary conversation, or, even worse, a talk session on the part of the interviewer. It is a common trap for the inexperienced interviewer to fall into—especially when dealing with the seasoned criminal.

DEALING WITH UNSATISFACTORY RESPONSES

Often an interviewer receives an answer which is:

1. Incomplete
2. Not correct
3. Not an answer to the question asked
4. Hostile
5. An expression of confusion as to what the interviewer means

When this difficulty occurs, the interviewer should attempt to deal with it by reevaluating the question to see whether it prompted the poor response by the way it was phrased. After doing so, he should seek to formulate the question once again. If a problem still exists in the way the person replies, steps should be taken to ensure that the individual realizes what is happening so the difficulty can be worked through with him.

Therefore, when recognizing that an inadequate response was given, an attempt should be made to find out what the source of the difficulty is as well as to obtain the answer to the question asked. It is indeed important for the interviewer to be aware not only of what the person does say, but also of what he doesn't say. The ability to recognize missing links in information and subsequently to follow them up and secure the needed data distinguishes the interviewer who has benefited from years of experience in the field. And so, though the new interviewer should try to be proficient in this area, he should not be discouraged if he does not immediately find himself able to notice when important information has been purposely omitted.

COMMONSENSE USE OF FREE ASSOCIATION

If one is able to recognize that a sufficient answer hasn't been provided and that the person is not purposely trying to conceal anything, a useful technique—especially for the inexperienced interviewer—is the commonsense use of free association. It can be used with a witness, for example, to aid him to recall the information required. The following questions illustrate how the technique of free association can be applied when interviewing a witness:

"What comes to your mind when you think of the robbery?"

"You mentioned that your neighbor was often drunk; can you tell me a little more about that?"

With this technique, the officer is presenting a familiar bit of information. Once the interviewee has this data, he is asked to think of it in an effort to trigger his recollection of other material associated with it, so that new information may be brought to light. The police often bring an individual back to the scene of a crime, a technique which brings the individual mentally into a certain area of information and is employed to find out whether seeing the physical surroundings will stimulate him to remember information previously not given. The same effect is being sought when an officer presents someone with a bit of information to try to uncover thoughts associated with it which would yield previously untapped clues.

In addition to its overall effectiveness, the adapted use of free association does not reveal how the officer feels about the subject; the question used is neutral. In the first example used above, "What comes to your mind when you think of the robbery?" the interviewer has not revealed how he feels about any of the circumstances surrounding the robbery. As a result, the commonsense use of free association can be a particularly useful and sophisticated tool to employ.

EVALUATING A POOR INTERVIEW

Despite all the tools for interviewing suggested in this chapter, inevitably a number of interviews will not turn out to the officer's satisfaction. If this happens, it will prove beneficial if he reflects on the interview session, shortly after it ends, to try to figure out what went wrong. A good way to do this, without wasting too much time, is for him to ask himself these four basic questions:

1. Did I say something to alienate the interviewee or to put him on the defensive?
2. Did I expect too much of the interview in the first place?
3. Did the interview get worse slowly, or did it go poorly after some particular point in the session?
4. Since the interview went poorly, what is my opinion of the interviewee? Do I think less of him now, which would therefore hamper my ability to interview him again without being impatient and hostile?

These questions should cover the primary causes for an unsatisfactory interview and should help the officer to evaluate accurately what went wrong and how it might be corrected.

TRANSITION

Thus far a number of interviewing techniques have been discussed. Before studying how to conclude an interview, there is one more technical aspect which requires the reader's attention. This area is the use of transitions in an interview.

As the interview moves along, a number of topics are usually discussed. During the session the interviewer can make the transition from one topic to another in three general ways: *gently*, *definitely*, and *sharply*.

When the transition is made *gently*, the least amount of stress is placed upon the interviewee. In this way the interviewer is allowing the individual to go at his own pace. The officer may either suggest a new area when the person is finished with one topic or say nothing at all, giving him the leeway to talk about whatever he wishes.

If the interviewer wants to move the session along more quickly, he can be more *definite* in getting the individual to move on to another subject. In this type of transition the officer interrupts the interviewee, describes what the person has been saying (thus saving time), and mentions another topic he wishes the person to discuss. The reader must realize, though, that in doing this to save time the interviewer may occasionally miss something the interviewee might have said if he hadn't been stopped.

Sharp transitions are usually employed in only two situations:

1. When the interviewee is becoming very anxious
2. When the interviewer is not getting anywhere with the interview

If an officer is interviewing a subordinate and sees that he is getting so upset that he is on the verge of "going to pieces," the best thing to do would be to immediately change the subject and come back to it later when the individual is more composed. It would be especially dangerous for an interviewer who was not a professional psychologist or psychiatrist to allow the interviewee to come close to a breakdown.

The other instance in which it's advantageous to use a sharp transition is when the interviewer is not getting anywhere with the interviewee. If an officer feels that this is the case, he may provoke the person by switching sharply from topic to topic. This technique should be used as a last resort, but it can be used effectively to cause an uncooperative person to be jarred out of his complacency.

A knowledge of the different types of transitions and when they should be used can be very helpful in making the sessions more effective. Haphazard jumping from topic to topic can significantly lower the success of the session.

CLOSING THE INTERVIEW

Much time has been devoted to the beginning and heart of the interview session. This final section notes two important points about the end of the interview:

1. No new material should be brought into the interview for discussion toward the end of the session.
2. Anxiety should be diminished toward the end of the interview.

If one is interviewing a subordinate concerning problems he is having on the job, one would want to impress him with the fact that he is being given proper attention. Furthermore, when he leaves the session, he should feel better, not worse. If new material is brought into the session toward the end, time will not be available to treat it fully, and the interviewee will have to be rushed, causing him to feel that the interviewer is not interested in his welfare.

The second point is self-explanatory. If the interviewee is anxious at the end of the session, he may very well leave with the feeling that nothing has been accomplished. On the other hand, if he leaves feeling better, he will consider that the interview was worthwhile. Therefore, the interviewer should try to diminish anxiety toward the end of the interview, specifically avoiding the treatment of anxiety-provoking subjects in the second half of the session.

WHAT WAS COVERED IN THIS CHAPTER

Since this chapter was designed to present a number of essential principles in interviewing, emphasis was placed on the importance of the interview relationship and the physical conditions under which the session is conducted. Also stressed were the need for privacy and the necessity of remembering what has been discussed in the event of an interruption, so that continuity is not hampered when the session is resumed.

Being able to adopt another person's internal frame of reference was cited as a necessary element in increasing one's understanding of the interviewee. Unless the officer is able to put himself in the interviewee's place, developing an understanding of him is practically impossible.

Attention was also given here to the role of silence in an interview. The following factors were given as possible reasons for an interviewee's silence:

1. The interviewee could be thinking about what he's going to say next.
2. He might be embarrassed about what has just been revealed to the interviewer.
3. He could be waiting to see the reaction of the interviewer to what he has said.
4. He might be expressing anger.
5. He might possibly be confused as to what he should say next.

In conjunction with a discussion of silence, the topic of nonverbal communication was treated as well. Voice tone, facial expression, and body gestures were noted as several ways in which people communicate information to one another. The officer was advised to be aware of what others are communicating nonverbally and to realize that he too is communicating information about himself in this way. The officer should generally use questions that are short, simple, neutral, and phrased in an indirect manner. This ensures that the interviewee is less likely to become defensive and is more open to further questioning.

Free association was described as a helpful method for the officer to use in interviewing. It is a neutral device in which one bit of information is presented to prompt recall of further data not previously mentioned.

One of the final topics covered on interviewing was the subject of transitions. Gentle transitions should incur the least amount of stress. Definite transitions can be used to save time and clarify what has been said to that point. And sharp transitions were noted as effective in curbing or causing anxiety, depending upon the type of person with whom they are used.

The reader should not expect to remember all the material on interviewing after only one reading. This chapter must be referred to again and again if the concepts are to be remembered easily enough to be used in one's daily activities. Furthermore, this chapter is just that—a chapter. Whole books have been written on interviewing. It is an extensive subject area which merits further study in depth. While the skills demonstrated here can greatly enhance the law enforcement officer's ability to interview, this chapter is still meant only as an introduction to the subject. A number of suggested texts on interviewing have been listed in the Selected Bibliography in the hope that students will be encouraged to read further on this topic.

REVIEW

1. What is an interview?
2. What important elements were mentioned in this chapter concerning the setting of the interview?
3. What is one particular way to enhance the development of an understanding of an interviewee?
4. What are five possible reasons for silence on the part of the interviewee during the session?
5. According to this chapter, what is a great block to the flow of communications between an interviewer and an interviewee?
6. In addition to verbal communication, what other type of communication is there during an interview?
7. If one needs to ask questions during an interview, what three words would best describe their makeup?
8. What four questions should one ask oneself when evaluating a poor interview?
9. What three types of transitions can be used in an interview, and when should they be employed?

chapter ten

Principles
in Interrogation

In the brief overview of the process called interviewing (Chapter 9), it was determined that interviewing is basically a method of gathering information. The law enforcement officer uses it with subordinates, witnesses, and parolees and in other instances where it is necessary for him to secure data.

Interrogation is also a method of gathering information. It is in fact a specific form of interviewing. However, since it is a particular type of interviewing process, its methodology is different in some ways. For example, interrogation is in contrast with basic interviewing in regard to (1) its purpose and (2) who employs it.

Whereas interviewing has as its goal to secure data, *interrogation is conducted either to get an admission of guilt from a person who has been involved in a crime or to obtain a clarification and elaboration of certain facts from someone who is innocent.* In other words, interviewing has a general purpose, but interrogation has a quite specific goal.

This difference points to the second area of contrast, namely, who employs interviewing and interrogation techniques. Since interviewing is a general process, it can be and is used by individuals in all walks of life. Those in government, industry, religion, and education as well as those in law enforcement employ interviewing. For the most part, this is not the case in the use of interrogation.

Historically, interrogation is an activity belonging to those in the field of law enforcement. As far back as the written word will attest, the man, agency, or state who made and enforced the laws also had the authority to interrogate the suspected and the guilty. This is still the case today.

Since this function is primarily borne by those in law enforcement, it particularly warrants the reader's attention. He is encouraged to absorb carefully the basic information presented in this chapter and also to delve into the principles of interrogation by proceeding to texts solely devoted to this subject.[1]

MIRANDA WARNINGS

Before the subject of interrogation is discussed, however, the officer must understand the following vital facts regarding the rights of a suspect. Their importance cannot be overemphasized.

Defendant's Right to Counsel. Of ever-increasing importance to the arrest procedure is the officer's responsibility to guarantee to the arrested his constitutional rights. This is a relatively new responsibility of the peace officer and has required a rather drastic change in his traditional role. As well as playing the part of an enforcer of the law, he must also be prepared to adequately protect the citizen from a deprivation of his basic rights. One of these rights is to be represented by an attorney.

There are some legal implications in these cases that demand constant attention. There is no need to provide the defendant with counsel immediately upon arrest, but he must be advised that he is entitled to an attorney and that if he is unable to obtain private counsel, he will be provided with one free of charge. Not only must he be advised of this, he must understand it. The officer must be prepared to show that such requirements have been met.

It goes without saying that under no conditions may the defendant be denied the right to seek, obtain, and talk to an attorney.

Defendant's Right to Remain Silent. In conjunction with and closely associated with his right to legal counsel, the defendant has also a definite right to remain silent in the face of the

---

[1] Fred E. Inbau and John E. Reid's *Criminal Interrogation and Confessions*, Williams and Wilkins, Baltimore, 1967, is a classic in this area; Arthur S. Aubry, Jr., and Rudolf R. Caputo's *Criminal Interrogation*, Charles C Thomson, Springfield, Ill., 1965, also presents an excellent treatment of the subject.

accusers. This guaranteed constitutional right also requires an admonition or warning on the part of arresting officers. Such a warning should be made verbally at the time of arrest and in writing at the time of booking. The important element here is that the defendant be made aware that he does not have to talk to anyone unless he wishes to do so and that anything he does say may be used against him in a court of law. Once again, his awareness must be coupled with understanding.

The Legal Admonishment. In an effort to standardize the legal requirements of the rights both to counsel and to silence, a warning or admonishment form has been devised and is being widely used. Such a form is necessary because of the precision on wording and understanding that is required by the courts. The face of the admonishment should substantially contain the four following phrases:

1. You have the right to remain silent.
2. Anything you say can and will be used against you in a court of law.
3. You have the right to talk to a lawyer and have him present with you while you are being questioned.
4. If you cannot afford to hire a lawyer, one will be appointed to represent you before any questioning, if you wish one.

These requirements are in no way meant to suppress the arrested person who wishes to talk to the investigators regarding the case. In order to protect the evidentiary value of the case, however, the arresting officers or follow-up investigators must obtain a waiver of his rights by the arrested. This can be accomplished by securing an affirmative reply, preferably in writing, to two questions, directly following the reading of the above warnings. These questions should be stated as follows:

1. Do you understand each of these rights I have explained to you?
2. Having these rights in mind, do you wish to talk to us now?

Having complied with this requirement, the investigation may progress as the case warrants. . . .

Confessions

Confessions and admissions are not ruled out by the constitutional right to remain silent and may properly be obtained as part of the arrest procedure. It is, however, imperative that the above legal admonishment be first given.

Second, it must be kept in mind that the confession must be given freely and voluntarily. The officer must always be able to produce proof that it was so given or realize that it will not be admissible in a court of law.[2]

GOALS OF INTERROGATION

The purpose of interrogation was said to be either (1) to get an admission of guilt from a person who has been involved in a crime or (2) to obtain a clarification and elaboration of certain facts from someone who is innocent. To accomplish this end more easily, there are a number of goals that the interrogator should keep in mind. If he does, he will be able to organize better his approach to the handling of the individual being interrogated so that he will not miss any areas likely to produce essential information.

The goals of interrogation can be broken down into two categories: primary and secondary. The primary goals are:

1. To ascertain *in detail* when and how the crime was executed
2. To find out how many individuals were involved and what part each of them played
3. To obtain enough data to lay the groundwork for future interrogation of the individual if it should be required
4. To narrow the search for the guilty person(s) by weeding out those suspects who are actually innocent

All of the above are areas in which the interrogator is naturally interested. He must find out how and when the crime was committed in detail so that a case can be developed against the person who is guilty. He must ensure not only that he has a guilty party, but that if there are others involved, they also are brought to justice. The purpose of law enforcement is not merely to catch a guilty person after a crime is committed, but to apprehend everyone who was involved.

In many cases one interrogation session is not sufficient to find the guilty party. In these instances the interrogator tries at least to eliminate suspects who are not guilty. In addition, he attempts to

---

[2] R. Gene Wright and John A. Marlo, *The Police Officer and Criminal Justice*, Copyright © McGraw-Hill, New York, 1970, pp. 184–186. Used with permission.

derive information which he can use in subsequent sessions. To have even a few details is profitable because the suspect can often be made to contradict himself if he is guilty. Furthermore, it is often the case that he cannot remember what he said in one session and will therefore be under greater pressure in a following meeting with the interrogation officer.

Once the primary goals are achieved or are almost within grasp, the secondary goals should be considered. These are:

1. To uncover any pattern of crimes in which the guilty person, his associates, or those for whom he works are currently or have been involved
2. To discover where any of the proceeds of the crime or criminal operation have been stored

These two goals, though termed "secondary," are essential for the investigator to keep in mind when conducting the interrogation. While the criminal is under duress, he will often reveal information on his other crimes or on the activities of others—facts he would not normally divulge if he had his guard up. It is also an opportune time to get any information on where the "take" has been stored, if it is that type of crime. Even if he has enough awareness not to reveal the location of the money or goods, he may well inadvertently give important clues as to their whereabouts.

If the interrogator is concentrating solely on a possible conviction, he may miss some information which the individual has unconsciously given. That is why the interrogator must be aware of the goals of interrogation. Carelessly missing information which could aid in the enforcement of the law and the prevention of future crimes because of poor organization is an affliction of amateurs, not professional peace officers. In order to be sure that he will not miss anything, therefore, the interrogator should properly prepare for the interrogation session.

PREPARING FOR THE INTERROGATION SESSION

In preparing for the session, the interrogator should call to mind the goals just enumerated, then he should familiarize himself with the facts of the case so he can deal confidently and intelligently with the suspect. The facts should revolve around two focal points: the crime and the criminal (or suspected criminal). The officer assigned to the interrogation will find that arranging the information this way will facilitate memorization. It can't be overemphasized that *a good memory is one of the primary assets of an adept interrogator.*

In reviewing the data which the department has on the crime itself, a number of questions and the known data should be well memorized. "Well memorized" means that the investigator should *overlearn* the facts which he is required to know. Overlearning is a technique in which the student continues to apply himself even when he believes he has mastered the material at hand. Thus when the interrogator feels he has the facts memorized, he should continue to study them. This will instill the information in his memory so he can recall it at will. This is important because timing is often a crucial element during the questioning period. If the interrogator hesitates too long while trying to recall a certain fact (in order to check what he knows with what the suspect has just said), the time lapse may cause him to lose the edge. A confident officer can apply pressure much better than one who is constantly groping for the facts he supposedly memorized.

The following is a partial list of questions which the interrogator should be able to answer concerning the crime, if the information is available, prior to beginning the interrogation:

When did the crime occur?
Where did it take place?
How does it appear the crime was committed?
How long does it seem to have taken for the crime to have been executed?
Were there any witnesses, and if so, what did they relate?
What could have been the motive for the crime?
What evidence was found at the scene of the crime?
How can the scene of the crime be described?
What factors point to the person being interrogated as being the guilty person?
Was the crime part of a pattern of crimes?
Who was the victim of the crime?
What information is available on the victim?
Why did the criminal choose to victimize him?

Without fail, then, the officer must be familiar with the circumstances of the crime in detail, assuming that they are available. Unfortunately, due to overconfidence, disinterest, or inexperience, the officer too often does not have all the necessary data within his grasp. This situation should be avoided at all costs.

Added to a knowledge of the answers to the above questions

concerning the crime, the officer should also have at his fingertips the following information concerning the criminal or suspected criminal whom he has been assigned to question. Most of it, naturally, is background information.

What is the correct spelling of the individual's name, and how is it pronounced?

What is the individual's marital status?

What is his physical condition?

What is known about his mental status?

What is his occupation?

How old is he?

Where does he live?

Does he know the victim?

Has he ever been in trouble before?

Approximately how much money does he earn?

Does he have any outstanding debts?

Are there any unusual activities in which he's involved?

Does he have any disreputable associates?

Does he use drugs or alcohol in excess?

Does he gamble?

Obviously, as in the previous set of questions on the circumstances of the crime, this list is only a partial one. However, it should give the reader an indication of the type of question he should be able to answer before he begins the interrogation.

If some of the facts which are necessary to answer these questions are not available, the officer should try to formulate possible hypotheses as to what the answers might be. These hypotheses should be *educated* guesses based on the evidence available. A hypothesis created from no information at all, or from personal biases, is not only useless but in some instances may even be harmful, for it can lead the investigator off the track. However, if enough material is present, the formulation of viable hypotheses is recommended.

INTERROGATION AREA

Part of the preparation for interrogation also involves providing a suitable place for holding the session, i.e., an interrogation room. Though most individuals know nothing about the principles of interrogation, many will be able to give a description of the interrogation scene as they see it. A sweating, *innocent victim* is pictured being subjected to lengthy, unduly harsh treatment by cruel interrogators in a room with barred windows and banks of hot glaring lights. As the reader no doubt realizes, this emotion-packed scene (though perpetuated by the entertainment media) is far from the real-life situation.

Today actual interrogation is done in an unobtrusive, quiet room that is adequately lighted. Even the barred windows are gone. If there are windows at all, they are usually covered with wire mesh. The trend now is to create a nonprison feeling in the interrogation room; the police and law enforcement atmosphere once considered necessary is now thought to be undesirable. In most cases, the interrogator is even dressed in civilian clothes to foster this effect.

Ideally the interrogation room should be soundproof so that no surrounding noises can serve as a distraction to either the interrogator or the suspect. Interruptions should be kept to a minimum, so that the mood which the officer creates in his questioning is not broken. Therefore, no phones should be located in the room, and associates should be informed when a session is going on so that they know not to walk in during the interrogation. As in interviewing, the fact that the session is held in a quiet place where there are no interruptions is extremely important. Privacy is often played down as a "nice-to-have" situation when questioning is being done. This is far from the truth. Suppose that you, the reader, were under interrogation. You would certainly not want to reveal anything within earshot of a large group of listeners. The interrogation room should be without noise or interference from outside.

The room should also be adequately lighted—not glaringly and not dimly, but well enough so that the officer can view the suspect. If the room is not illuminated brightly enough, the officer will not be able to observe the nonverbal information which the suspect is communicating to him (see Chapter 9). If it's too well lit, the individual may feel that he is about to get the "third degree," which would put him especially on guard and thus hostile to the interrogator.

HANDLING THE SUSPECT

How well the suspect is handled during the session will obviously affect the degree of success achieved. Two main elements that are worthy of attention are:

1. Technique employed in questioning the suspect
2. How the interrogator presents himself to the person being interrogated

Since the first of these will be covered in detail later in the chapter, we shall turn to the second element and analyze it briefly.

There are a number of points an officer should remember so that he will present the correct image during the interrogation session. However, the overall factor under which all of them can be listed is *professionalism*. If an officer conducts the session as a professional, he will definitely improve his chances of success. Professionalism embodies many things for many people, so it would be beneficial to list a few of the traits which are implied by it and which should be present in a good interrogator:

1. Confidence
2. Patience
3. Dedication
4. Straightforwardness

If the interrogator shows evidence of lacking confidence, getting a confession will be an uphill battle. The suspect will be convinced that he has a chance because there isn't enough evidence against him and that the interrogating officer cannot keep up a front as long as he because the officer is not sure of the case against him.

Lack of patience can probably cause just as much harm as a deficiency in confidence. Once again the suspect will be inclined to believe that he can be stronger than the interrogator and will thus try to wait him out. The officer should take pains not to show he is impatient by squirming in his chair or pacing in the room. When the interrogator becomes jittery and annoyed, he is saying in essence, "He (the suspect) has gotten the better of me." And so, impatience and lack of confidence have no place in the interrogation room.

Dedication, another element of professionalism, is another important trait for the interrogator to portray. If the suspect feels that the officer is dedicated and motivated, he is more likely to give in than if he feels that the officer lacks interest in the case and will give up sooner or later. The suspect must be made to feel that the officer is going to stay with it to the end. Expressions of boredom on the part of the interrogator are usually an indication to the suspect that the end may be in sight. This feeling must never be fostered, otherwise the session may be lengthened because of it; in some cases it may even result in the suspect's becoming so encouraged by what he sees as a weak interrogator that he may never give in!

Straightforwardness is equally desirable in an interrogator. If the officer is able to treat the suspect without disdain and to question him in a nonemotional way, the individual may feel that he is being dealt with fairly—that the officer is not out to "get" him but to see that justice is done. When the suspect is not treated as a man but is subjected to verbal abuse and innuendos, he may become quite hostile. Furthermore, he may feel that the officer does not have a case against him and that he's trying to "sweat" a confession out of him. This is why it is preferable not to use emotion-laden words in the questioning, such as steal, kill, or mug, but instead to use neutral terms like take, shoot, or hit. By dealing with the individual respectfully and clinically (as opposed to emotionally), the results should prove to be more productive.

Having discussed the image of the interrogator and its effect on the outcome of the session, the chapter will conclude by describing a number of particular techniques which can be applied during the session.

METHODS OF APPROACH IN INTERROGATION

The particular techniques which can be applied during the interrogation session can be divided into two broad categories: the direct approach and the indirect approach. As categories they will sometimes overlap, but one should still be able to see why a certain method was assigned to one or the other of these two headings.

The direct approach is characterized by an attitude on the part of the officer that the suspect is surely guilty and that various factors point to this belief. On the other hand, the indirect approach focuses on the use of sympathy and other varied techniques which would allow the interrogator to "get his foot in the door" and cause the suspect to make some type of admission of guilt.

Direct Approach in Interrogation

In the direct approach there are three primary techniques which the officer can employ. They are:

1. Demonstrate to the suspect that you are firmly convinced that he is guilty.
2. Inform him that his attitude and reactions to the accusation that he is guilty attest to his involvement in the crime.
3. Indicate to him *some* of the circumstantial evidence which proves his guilt.

Being firmly convinced that the suspect is guilty is important, but the officer should not be "cocky" in his attitude. To say, "Look, buddy, I know you're guilty as sin, so you'd better admit it" accomplishes little and may even cause the suspect to become more stubborn. Instead, the officer might say something along these lines: "I'm confident that you're guilty because of all the factors involved—evidence we now have and material which has just come to light; it would be to your best interest to confess rather than to let yourself in for more trouble and aggravation."

How one reacts to the comments of the suspect, as well as what one says, is another important element. For example, if the individual begins to declare his innocence, it will affect him if the officer shakes his head from side to side, indicating that he doesn't believe it. Some experts in the field of interrogation also feel that the officer should cut off the suspect when he tries to protest his innocence, because if he is continually allowed to proclaim that he is not guilty, it will be harder for him later to indicate to the interrogator that he lied previously and was actually guilty.[3]

To point out that he is further convinced of the suspect's guilt, the officer can indicate to him that he is even acting as a guilty person does. Nervous, sweating, confused—the officer need only make the suspect realize these labels fit him and he is likely to become more upset emotionally, thus manifesting these signs in a more pronounced way than before and causing increased stress, which will make him more amenable to confessing his crime. Moreover, he will be convinced that his guilt is indeed showing.

The other direct approach mentioned above was to indicate to the suspect *some* of the circumstantial evidence that the force already has against him. In this way, it is hoped, the suspect will come to believe that it's only a matter of time before there will be enough evidence to convict him or that there already is enough to put him in jail. However, in most circumstances the officer shouldn't reveal all circumstantial evidence to the suspect. Doing this puts the interrogator at a disadvantage since he no longer has any element of surprise or leverage which he can bank on if the suspect does not give in and confess. Therefore, a general rule of thumb would be *never* to reveal all the circumstantial evidence one has against the suspect. If the situation calls for it, some might be revealed, but even in cases of that nature all the data possessed should not be disclosed. This point is important.

Indirect Approach

By way of introduction to some techniques in this category (indirect approach), a hypothetical statement by an interrogator to a

[3] Inbau and Reid, *op. cit.*, p. 31.

rape suspect will be presented to illustrate the indirect approach. The setting is an interrogation room, and the suspect, Mark L., has been brought in on a rape charge along with two of his companions. Mark is being interrogated alone.

Mark, you're here on a rape charge. Just looking at the facts in the case, rape seems like a pretty harsh charge for what I think probably happened. Let me reconstruct the scene, and after I've finished tell me if it wasn't the way I've described it.

It was about ten o'clock and you saw Helen S. leave the dance by herself. She'd been flirting with you, Bill, and Tom all evening. The three of you decided to follow her out. When the three of you got outside, you decided to see if her flirting meant anything. You walked up to her near an alley and one of the other fellows suggested the three of you have a little fun. She seemed to resist you, but you felt that it was all part of the game, like when she taunted the three of you at the dance. After it was all over, she decided to get back at you for accidentally hurting her a little and reported you to the police. Isn't that the way it was, or did I miss something?

In the above situation, the interrogator did the following things:

1. He attempted to lessen the severity of the crime in the eyes of the suspect by claiming it didn't seem too serious to him (the interrogator).
2. He brought Mark back to the scene of the crime.
3. He pushed most of the blame for the offense on the victim and the other two youths.
4. He made many occurrences sound as if they were accidental, not purposeful.

By lessening the magnitude of the crime in the suspect's eyes, that is, by saying he didn't think the crime was quite what it was made out to be, the interrogator is able to enhance the chances that the suspect will confess; two possible results are:

1. Mark will feel less guilty about the crime and consider it not a very horrible thing to confess to after all.
2. Mark will feel that the interrogator won't think less of him if he confesses; he doesn't feel threatened by the officer.

The second technique used was to bring the suspect back to the scene of the crime. Doing this will often precipitate a confession from the suspect—especially if he is apprehended soon after the crime. (Incidentally, if the officer is in doubt about the suspect's guilt, this is an excellent way to observe the person to see whether he shows some reaction when brought back to where the crime occurred.)

Pushing the blame for the crime onto the shoulders of the victim and the accomplices was the third technique employed by the interrogator. Its effect on the suspect is similar to the effect of the first technique. It also serves to drive a wedge between one suspect and the others involved in the crime. In some crimes—murder and robbery—this can be even further developed by playing one suspect against another.

The final specific technique employed in dealing with Mark L. was to make the occurrences sound like the result of accidental events, so that the crime would not seem planned. The reason for this is to get the individual to feel that he was a victim of circumstance, whether this is actually the case or not, so that he will be even more inclined to confess since it really wasn't *completely* his fault.

In addition to the specific roles played by the techniques used above, in combination they also have a general effect which is beneficial to the interrogator. They tend to draw the officer and the suspect closer together. This happens when the interrogator appears to be taking the suspect's side by lessening the crime and the person's role in it. Therefore, if interrogation techniques are used properly, they can make the officer's job much easier—all it takes is patience and perseverance.

INTERROGATING INDIVIDUALS WHOSE GUILT IS UNKNOWN OR DOUBTFUL

The above techniques were samples of the type used when the suspect's guilt seems quite certain. However, there are many instances when an officer must interrogate a suspect whose guilt is unknown or doubtful. There are usually two main reasons for this:

1. He does not have all the information on the case.
2. The suspect has not revealed data which would tip off the interrogator.

So, essentially, the interrogator does not know whether the suspect is guilty or not because he has not got sufficient evidence to make an educated guess. The steps he must take should therefore focus on getting more information from the suspect under interrogation. This process can simply be a matter of refreshing the person's memory, if he's innocent, or forcing him to slip, as in the case of a guilty person.

If the interrogator wants to assume that the suspect is innocent, he can approach the individual in the following ways to elicit more information from him:

1. Have him relate again what he knows about the crime and the victim.
2. Ask him to go over again his whereabouts and actions on the day of the crime.

In the above approaches the officer is not trying to trap the suspect; he is merely trying to obtain information from him which had been glossed over in the previous session or sessions. It is often true that in subsequent sessions information which was thought to be unimportant by the suspect or the officer (or both) takes on a new dimension and brings a different side of the case to light.

The above method of dealing with a suspect for the first time or in a follow-up session was utilized to seek more general information; but the interrogator can also try to trick the suspect in an effort to see whether he's actually innocent. In this method of interrogation, the officer can use the following techniques:

1. Ask questions to which the answers are already known, to see whether he's lying.
2. Present fabricated data on the case to see how the individual deals with it.

These two oblique ways of seeing whether the individual is lying should give the officer an opportunity to make a better evaluation of the situation. With the above techniques, as with all the others presented in this chapter, the interrogator is trying to get the suspect to tell the truth in its entirety. When this happens, the guilty can be tried and the innocent set free.

WHAT WAS COVERED IN THIS CHAPTER

The principles of interrogation were introduced to the reader in this chapter. It differs from interviewing in that its purpose is more specific. The purpose of interrogation is either to get an admission of guilt from a person who has been involved in a crime or to obtain a clarification and elaboration of certain facts from someone who is innocent.

Emphasis was placed once again on the importance of the proper physical setting for interrogation, as it was for interviewing. However, some guidelines were added this time for the officer to follow if his memory is to serve him during the session. He should overlearn the necessary material, so as to minimize the possibility of a lapse in memory when the pressure is on to have the facts at one's fingertips.

Also brought out here was the point that an interrogator must manifest professionalism at all times. Under this general concept were listed the traits of confidence, patience, dedication, and straightforwardness. Without these traits an officer cannot expect to become a successful interrogator.

The direct and indirect approaches to interrogation were also presented in this chapter. In the direct approach there are three primary techniques which the officer can employ:

1. Demonstrate to the subject that you are firmly convinced of his guilt.
2. Inform his that his attitude and reactions to the accusation that he is guilty attest to his involvement in the crime.
3. Indicate to him *some* of the circumstantial evidence which proves his guilt.

In the indirect approach, some of the techniques mentioned were bringing the suspect back to the scene of the crime; lessening the magnitude of the crime; pushing the blame onto the suspect's companions; and making the crime sound more accidental than purposeful.

The final area covered concerned the questioning of suspects whose guilt was unknown or doubtful. Techniques such as (1) asking questions to which the answers are already known, and (2) the fabrication of data to observe whether the person will lie are among the types used in these situations.

Since interrogation is especially important for those in law enforcement, emphasis was also placed on the need for the reader to pursue this topic further in other texts solely devoted to criminal interrogation.

The word "interrogation" has long had a negative connotation in most people's minds, probably because of the cunning with which it must be used for it to be successful. Yet, like a firearm, interrogation is a necessary tool of law enforcement officers. And like a firearm it must be used with care, since it will help the officer only if he is prepared to employ it through constant practice.

REVIEW

1. How does interrogation differ from interviewing?
2. What is the definition of interrogation?
3. What are four goals of interrogation?
4. Describe an ideal interrogation room.
5. What are four traits of a good interrogator?
6. How does the direct approach to interrogation differ from the indirect approach?
7. According to this chapter, what is one of the primary assets of an adept interrogator?

section four

Psychology, Law Enforcement, and Corrections

chapter eleven

Psychology behind Bars: The Role of the Correctional Psychologist

Jail, brig, prison, penitentiary, stockade—grim words that bring to one's mind the image of an overcrowded, dark, damp, dingy, foreboding structure. In this ugly setting could there possibly be some type of work for the psychologist to do? Is there a place for the use of psychological tools alongside the restraining belts and handcuffs? The answer is a definite yes, according to judges, sheriffs, correction officers, criminals, sociologists, the clergy, and practically everyone today.

Recognition is now widespread that punishment, much less punishment by itself, is almost useless as a corrective measure. The approach presently being emphasized is described in the following definition taken from the *American Association of Correctional Psychologists' By-Laws:*

> Correctional psychology is the study and application of psychological knowledge in the administration of criminal justice. This knowledge may relate to any or all of the points in time during which a lawbreaker is identified, tried, institutionalized or released. The goals of correctional psychology are to seek means of understanding offender behavior, to aid offenders in achieving more effective intellectual, social or emotional functioning, and to promote more successful societal adjustment of offenders.[1]

[1] *American Association of Correctional Psychologists' By-Laws*, Article III.

151

It is not true, as often claimed by the few opponents of the new principles of penology, that "coddling" is a goal of correctional psychology. What is actually happening is that various techniques never tried before are being employed in an effort to return the criminal to society, never to be imprisoned again.

Obviously psychologists have their work cut out for them. The recidivism rate is so high now in some areas that the odds favor almost immediate reconfinement for those presently being released from prison. Is it any wonder, then, that penitentiaries are over-crowded? Moreover, since the population is spiraling upward, in the not-too-distant future the institutions will be even more crammed. Couple these conditions with the high cost of rising crime, and the need for advancement in rehabilitation of criminal offenders becomes quite urgent.

With the need for progressive penology made evident, this chapter will explore the manner in which the psychologist contributes to the correctional process. His role will be broken down into two main functions: working with the facility's staff and dealing directly with the confinees. Since there is a shortage of professionals such as psychologists due to budgetary restrictions as well as to the inadequate supply present to meet increasing demands, the necessary emphasis is on the psychologist's staff training role rather than his duties in working with the prisoners.

It is hoped that this situation will soon be alleviated. Funds are now being made available by the federal and state governments in ever-increasing amounts. In addition, organizations such as the American Correctional Association and the American Association of Correctional Psychologists have made immense contributions in uplifting professionalism in this field. At this point, the work performed by a correctional psychologist with the staff members of penal institutions will be examined.

THE PSYCHOLOGIST AND THE SECURITY STAFF

Though the psychologist works hard and long with the treatment staff, since they are his primary concern, he must also spend some time with the security staff. The security staff must be aware of what the treatment personnel are trying to accomplish; if they aren't, the two groups may eventually be working against each other instead of as a team. Ignorance of what the counselors are trying to achieve and a poor understanding of the rehabilitation process can cause unnecessary friction between a guard and a counselor, just as a lack of familiarity with security principles by those in the treatment field could cause avoidable difficulties. The prison psychologist should therefore ensure that the programs he is involved in are properly publicized with respect to their purpose, methods, and scheduling.

Another duty the psychologist performs for those involved in security is to teach classes in human behavior. This is done on a preservice and an ongoing in-service basis. Since the correction officer has more contact with the prisoners than does the counselor or the psychologist, it is essential that some principles of psychology be disseminated to the correction officers. Of course, the classes would be conducted on a different plane, and the level of instruction would be simpler than in the classes taught to the counselors.

However, important techniques and basic concepts are beneficial to those in security. Since the correction officers, as noted previously, have more contact with the prisoners, it is desirable to make the security personnel part of the therapeutic community which the psychologist is trying to set up within the prison framework. It's perfectly possible for the right type of person on the security force, with the proper training, to do more to affect the confinees' life than a trained counselor. Therefore, the correctional psychologist usually has an extensive program for the "nontreatment staff" who are performing security functions.

One other aid he often provides for the prison warden is to screen the applicants for security positions. An interview and battery of personality and intelligence tests are administered to determine whether the candidate is suitable for correctional work. In addition, the psychologist can also use a follow-up procedure if time and manpower permit. In the follow-up, he reinterviews and retests the personnel to check whether they are:

1. Having personality problems
2. In need of a change in assignment
3. Becoming callous toward the prisoners
4. Losing their patience because they are under too much pressure

The correctional psychologist is thus concerned with screening, training, and reevaluating security personnel. The belief held by some that the psychologist is out to find flaws in an individual's personality as grounds for firing him is simply untrue.

In a psychological screening, he is trying to find out whether the applicant is suitable and will be comfortable in the corrections field. He's not out to prevent the individual from getting the job; rather he is trying to ensure that the applicant is not making a mistake. It is far better for the candidate to be advised as to his incompatibility before he takes the job, so that a nervous breakdown two years hence may be avoided. Furthermore, when the psychologist reexamines a guard in a follow-up interview, he is seeking to help the individual in his work.

If a transfer from an exterior post to an interior one or vice versa is indicated, a psychologist might be able to spot it and recommend that the change be enacted to assist the correction officer. A change like this, though it sounds inconsequential, could mean the difference between staying in corrections or having to quit. So the psychologist, if anything, is out to assist the security staff by working closely with them.

TESTING AND INTERVIEWING THE PRISONERS

As mentioned at the beginning of the chapter, the ideal situation is one where the correctional psychologist works personally with the prisoners. Yet in many instances this is not possible because of a shortage of funds and personnel. However, the situation in a growing number of facilities is rapidly improving to the point where the psychologist has a great deal of contact with the prisoners. Therefore, this area especially merits close attention.

When a person is first confined, prison authorities need to know some basic facts about him. For example, it would be helpful to have:

1. A gross impression of him
2. Some idea of his personality status
3. An estimate of his educational level
4. An indication of the field of work he is interested in

To get a gross impression of him, the psychologist seeks to find out how bright the individual is, what his vocational aspirations are, and what his mental status is. This information aids the treatment and security staff to understand him and make intelligent decisions concerning his custody classification as well as the type of program to which he should be assigned.

As a result, the techniques used to find out the confinee's mental status are important. If an individual is unfit for confinement because he is psychotic, this must be spotted as soon as possible. To accomplish this the psychologist can use either a projective or an objective personality test (see Chapter 2). Presently the trend is toward the use of the Minnesota Multiphasic Personality Inventory (MMPI), and research is currently being done to make its use in corrections more fruitful. However, projective tests such as the Rorschach and the Thematic Apperception Test (TAT) are still in wide use. An intake interview by a psychologist usually accompanies this type of test to supplement its findings. The diagnosis that results is then made a permanent part of the prisoner's file.

In a number of facilities, the personality status test is only part of a battery of tests. Aptitude, achievement, and vocational tests are also given to increase the amount of data with which to make professional judgments. The aptitude and achievement tests, for example, give the staff an indication of the confinee's educational level as well as his potential. In addition, they identify the rare cases in which the individual is not trainable or educable.

A high school achievement test is an especially valuable tool because it gives the tester an indication of the work the prisoner should be assigned to in the correctional facility's school. A major problem of many adolescents who had trouble in school is that they were pushed through too fast. In a correctional facility, however, the individual is given a grade level on the basis of his score on an achievement test. A prisoner could be placed in grade 8 even though he might previously have reached the eleventh grade before dropping out of school. By doing this, and by allowing him to progress at his own pace, the institution hopes to avoid unnecessary frustrations, thus improving the chances that he will receive his diploma.

An aptitude or intelligence test which would give the psychologist the prisoner's IQ is helpful as well. By knowing what his potential is, the staff is able to match it with his performance level in class to see whether he is working up to his capacity. If he isn't, it could be the result of a lack of motivation, and this is an area for the confinee's counselor to work out with him.

Vocational tests can also be part of the battery of tests given to new confinees. Though the validity and reliability of most tests of this type are still questionable, they can, at the very least, be used to promote the success of an interview related to the prisoner's vocational goals. It is indeed an important part of the rehabilitative process to discuss with the individual his future plans. Therefore, if for no other reason, vocational tests can be employed as a means to ascertain what the prisoner's vocational interests and abilities seem to be.

In addition to formal tests such as those discussed above, a questionnaire could be used. A locally prepared, short, sentence-completion questionnaire could be quite effective in determining:

1. The prisoner's ability to write and think coherently
2. His interest areas
3. Some of his surface feelings on basic social issues

The following four lines which the confinee could be asked to complete illustrate the kind of subject that could be touched upon in a questionnaire:

1. Four jobs I'd like to have are:
   a._____ b._____
   c._____ d._____
2. I hate people who_____.
3. In my spare time I_____.
4. People should always _____.

Once again, though, as in the case of projective and vocational tests, the questionnaire might be quite unreliable and invalid if used by itself; but it can be effectively employed as a point of departure in a counseling session. Therefore, it can be quite a useful tool if it is given in conjunction with an interview.

There are three other areas in which techniques of measurement can aid the psychologist. They are:

1. Assigning to a prisoner a proper security classification
2. Deciding what type of work assignments a confinee should have
3. Determining who an inmate's counselor should be

Since the immediate aim of a correctional facility is security, the careful designation of a suitable custody classification to each prisoner is essential. Testing and interviewing aids the staff in assigning prisoners a correct classification just as it assisted the treatment staff to determine a program for them. For instance, if a prisoner was diagnosed as a suicide risk, he could be classified as a maximum security prisoner and sent to administrative segregation. In this special cell he could be observed closely so that he wouldn't be able to take his own life as an easy way out. He would remain in this status until proper psychological treatment improved his outlook.

Another pertinent example concerns the diagnosis of homosexuality. If the tests and interview results indicate that a woman prisoner is a lesbian, she can be classified accordingly and sent to a special dorm or an individual cell, depending on the procedures of the facility. Both examples illustrate how proper custody classification of prisoners depends on accurate testing and interview procedures.

When a work assignment is made, many things have to be taken into account, but one of the primary decisions concerns whether the prisoner should work inside or outside the facility. The psychologist's personality status test and interview should produce data that can help determine the stability and attitude of a prisoner so that an educated guess may be made as to whether the confinee would attempt to escape. In addition, the interview and tests should provide information which the counselor can use in selecting a trade for the prisoner in the prison shops.

Many types of prisoners are processed into prisons daily. In large facilities a number of counselors are usually employed. During the initial classification stage, since the psychologist is familiar with both the counselors' abilities and personalities, as well as the incoming prisoners' assets and liabilities, he can assign each prisoner to a counselor who might be particularly suited to deal with him. This is an especially important function because much time can be saved, and the interviews can be considerably more productive, if the counselor chosen for an inmate is "right" for him. To appreciate this, one need only think of one's own associates; some, no doubt, can be talked to freely, but there are probably others one can hardly pass the time of day with. When assigning a counselor, the psychologist is involved in a decision which could be very significant in the rehabilitation of the prisoner.

In essence, then, testing and interviewing are utilized to aid the correctional psychologist in making educated guesses concerning new confinees. In addition, there are some indirect benefits from the tests; their use often impresses the new prisoner with the belief that somebody is really interested in him now. Furthermore, the complex screening processes that many facilities have may even give the new confinee some assurance that he is going to be helped while incarcerated.

With these points in mind, interviewing and testing services in penal institutions under the direction of a correctional psychologist are now being expanded at an accelerated pace. It has at last become apparent to those in supervisory capacities that much can be done for today's prison population on the basis of the information gathered during the screening process.

CURRENT METHODS OF TREATMENT

Once initial classification has been completed, treatment to correct the offender begins. The methods employed to accomplish rehabilitation are designed to aid the confinee to become more productive while incarcerated and, upon release, to enable him to fill a more acceptable role as a useful member of society. However, this philosophy of treatment is not always seen as desirable by everyone.

After someone has committed a crime, many persons—including those involved directly in law enforcement and prison security—find it hard to accept the fact that a lawbreaker should be given any treatment other than punishment. Punishment for the offense in the form of hard work is often cited as being the ideal treatment.

Yet, as was mentioned earlier in the chapter, punishment has almost no corrective effect. By contrast, positive treatment approaches offer at least some hope when applied to the task of correcting antisocial behavior.

Rehabilitative efforts have a purpose, then, namely, to correct. They are not used to pacify or "coddle" the prisoner, as is sometimes incorrectly believed.

This appreciation of the true purpose of rehabilitative techniques must be understood and accepted by the correction officer, if correctional psychology is to stem the increase in recidivism. Otherwise, the treatment staff will only be working at odds with the security personnel. And the two staffs must work as a team if effective treatment is to be possible.

An essential part of the correction of prisoners is the vocational training and educational program. In the attempt to provide the individual offender with several tools he can use to financially and socially break the bonds of poverty without resorting to crime, formal education is provided. He is encouraged to obtain his high school diploma or take college-level courses (if available) while in prison. In addition, he is usually given the opportunity to become proficient in a new trade. Both vocational and educational training should aid him to become more physically self-sufficient.

Added to the above training, the offender may also undergo psychological treatment in the form of therapy. Therapy is an intensified form of counseling. It is a method in which a person can work out his problems and learn new approaches to life. Therapy can be conducted on a one-to-one basis or in a group.

As well as being trained and possibly involved in therapy, the confinee in most penal institutions takes part in an ongoing classifica-

tion program. In a classification program there are a number of
levels. Each succeeding level has a greater amount of privileges and
allots more freedom to the confinee. As a prisoner begins to work
out his problems and indicates through his behavior that he is able to
act in an acceptable manner on a particular level, he is reclassified to
a new level.

This assignment to a new classification is a reward for behaving
properly. Ideally, since his good behavior is reinforced, he should
want to continue to demonstrate that he can handle the new free-
doms he is given so he will be given more freedom. Reclassification, a
process in which he is gradually given more and more freedom, ends
when he is finally given almost complete freedom in the form of
parole. By the time he reaches this stage, it is hoped, the reinforced
socially acceptable behavior will have become part of his makeup and
will offset his urge to return to crime.

SOME ADDITIONAL FUNCTIONS OF THE CORRECTIONAL PSYCHOLOGIST

Added to the training of the staff, the testing and interviewing of
prisoners, and his involvement in the classification process, there are
a number of other functions a correctional psychologist can perform.
For example, he can:

1. Act as consultant to the parole board
2. Coordinate treatment activities with key staff members
3. Evaluate the mood of the inmate population

As a consultant to the parole board he can advise the officials
involved concerning the attitude of the prisoner; in some instances he
may make a specific suggestion, such as that the confinee should be
released on parole under the condition that he attend psychotherapy
on a regular basis.

Coordination must take place with certain key personnel, or the
psychologist's program may interfere with other staff personnel's
roles. Moreover, good ideas are passed among the staff members
during these meetings, and teamwork results when the lines of communication are open. The correctional psychologist should coordinate primarily with the persons filling the following billets:

1. Warden
2. Medical officer

3. Chaplain
4. Classification officer

Taking all of the functions of the prison psychologist into account, one can see that he comes into constant close contact with both the staff and the confinees. As a result, he is able to—and should—keep his finger on the pulse of the inmate population. This is beneficial because in this capacity he can advise the warden when unrest is brewing and when staff problems are evident. With this knowledge unnecessary incidents can often be avoided, and difficulties can be corrected before they become major problems.

WHAT WAS COVERED IN THIS CHAPTER

It should be evident from this chapter that the correctional psychologist has an important place in the successful operation of a penal institution. He is involved in the classification of new inmates. Through testing and interviewing, he and his staff obtain information which makes prisoner assignment a more objective process, thus increasing the accuracy with which it is carried out.

In addition to the psychologist's work with classification of new prisoners, he is also responsible for the functioning of the treatment program. In this program, the confinee is taught to become a productive citizen through:

1. Occupational training
2. Therapy, in which the inmate is given a chance to become involved with the psychologist, or a member of his staff, in order to relearn how to deal with life without resorting to drugs or crime
3. Participation in an ongoing classification program, in which the prisoner is given more freedom as and when he shows an ability to handle more

As well as working with the prisoners, the psychologist has the responsible duty of working with the staff. Usually he is expected to screen new officers coming in to determine whether they have any gross personality defects which would disqualify them for stressful work with a criminal population. Furthermore, he is often called upon to reevaluate officers to see whether they need a change of post or assignment.

The correctional psychologist today has a more important role than ever before in the field of corrections. He is expected to work with both the security and treatment staffs. He must also be aware of the entire prisoner treatment program, from initial classification to final parole decisions.

Today, the weight of making the corrections process successful is placed, to a great degree, on the shoulders of the correctional psychologist. How the psychologist bears this burden will determine the future direction of prisoner rehabilitation.

REVIEW

1. Give the main elements of the definition of correctional psychology according to the American Association of Correctional Psychologists.
2. What are four reasons why a psychologist would retest and have a follow-up interview with a correction officer after he has been on the job for a year?
3. In the classification of new inmates, what information does the correctional psychologist seek to obtain?
4. Why is it true that punishment, of itself, is almost useless as a corrective measure?
5. What type of tests can correctional psychologists give to new prisoners in the reception phase?
6. Discuss why treatment, instead of punishment, is necessary if criminals are to become productive members of society.
7. What are some of the additional functions of the correctional psychologist as indicated in this chapter?
8. Who are the individuals with whom the correctional psychologist should coordinate?
9. What is the purpose of the reclassification of prisoners to a new level in which they would have more freedom?

chapter twelve

On the Road
with Psychology

Mention driving to many people today, and pleasure doesn't even come to mind. The thought of a quiet, relaxing drive in the country doesn't strike a familiar chord anymore. To motorists, driving means heavy traffic, speeding tickets, horrible accidents, costly repairs, and possible death. Driving has indeed become a dangerous business. Speed is a way of life, powerful cars an accepted fact.

Since the race to the hospital and the grave by careless drivers is occurring more frequently, law enforcement agencies are now putting greater and greater stress on accident prevention programs. Summonses are being given by the thousands each day. Safe driving lectures are held daily throughout the nation. Traffic engineers are desperately searching for better techniques to improve future roads and eliminate old hazards. The problems of accident prevention are being tackled from all angles. Furthermore, as an understanding of the problems involved increases, more extensive measures will be taken.

Psychology has much to offer in the field of traffic safety. Information provided by trained observers such as psychologists can help those in law enforcement and safety to:

1. Understand more clearly why people speed and drive carelessly
2. Find more efficient ways of enforcing regulations and saving lives
3. Realize how violators should be handled

163

4. Design safer highways and develop effective road signs
5. Meaningfully teach safe driving classes

WHY PEOPLE TAKE CHANCES: THE PSYCHOLOGY OF SPEEDERS AND CARELESS DRIVERS

Death is permanent. Speeding seems immature and careless driving foolish. In most instances drivers are aware of what terrible ends they can meet, yet they continue to challenge the odds. This being the case, one is bound to wonder why people take such unnecessary chances on the road.

There are a number of factors which might help provide an answer. This chapter will cover six of them:

1. The mental state of the driver
2. The motorist's physical condition
3. The insecurity or immaturity of the driver
4. The motorist's intellectual ability
5. Inattention while behind the wheel
6. Driving and false security

The Mental State of the Driver

Angry, happy, frustrated, upset—the motorist can be in any of these emotional states when he's behind the wheel. People often drive when weighed down by many problems or "in seventh heaven" because of recent good news. It is common knowledge that few drivers are completely calm, cool, and collected when traveling. Usually our feelings are colored by the day's activities. We may be depressed, or greatly overjoyed. How we feel varies greatly from one time to another, but frequently we are not fully composed. It's only human to experience life with some emotion. However, even though emotionality is normal, it can result in a normally competent driver becoming involved in an accident.

A young man's new bride is sick with pneumonia. He is driving to the hospital to visit her after work. He's quite upset not only because she's ill, but also because he doesn't have hospitalization coverage. Instead of paying attention to the road, he is concentrating on how he can solve his financial problem. While he's involved in working out this difficulty, his car slowly inches over into the other lane. Seconds later a solution is provided for him. He dies on impact from a head-on collision.

Paul T. receives good news in the mail. Excited and thrilled over his good fortune, he jumps in the car to rush over to his aunt's house to tell her about it. As he is driving on the highway, he doesn't realize that the rise in his emotional level has been matched by an increase in the speed at which he's driving. He attempts too late to slow down while exiting from the highway; his car spins, topples, and crashes. He will never deliver the news to his aunt.

Long-time residents of a particular small town are prejudiced against Jim S. because he has lived there for only two years. He's frustrated about not making any progress in his job at the local factory. One day after work he pulls out onto the expressway which is only a mile from where he's employed. Still angry about the conditions in the factory, he displaces the hostility he has toward his boss, to whom he cannot show anger, onto other motorists. First he begins tailing an old model car in the right lane, then he pulls out into the passing lane and slows down to 5 miles per hour below the speed limit. A driver behind him going at the speed limit blinks his lights as a signal for him to pull over so he can pass. The frustrated factory worker ignores him. A state patrolman in an unmarked car observes the incident and pulls over the frustrated driver. Now he's not only frustrated, but he's out a $25 fine as well.

Every day people lose control of their judgment and their vehicles because of emotionality. These incidents have been presented to re-emphasize that when one is behind the wheel, driving is a full-time job. One must remember this fact not only when teaching a driving safety course, but also when emotionally upset and behind the wheel of a car.

Law enforcement officers may be killed just as easily as other people. This statement may seem silly, but it's often forgotten. In today's society the law enforcement officer does more driving than the average person. Also he is involved in emotionally charged situations at every turn. These two elements are the main ingredients in many auto fatalities.

One may not always be able to prevent himself from getting angry, and hearing good news should make a person happy. However, the motorist should be aware of how he feels when getting behind the wheel so he can make a special effort to pay attention to what he's doing. The reader must understand this point and make others realize it as well. How well this is remembered can make the difference between dying today and living to drive tomorrow.

Physical Condition of the Driver

Fatigue, drugs and alcohol, hunger, age, and deficiencies in vision can adversely affect one's driving performance just as significantly as one's mental attitude. Physical drives and inadequacies may greatly diminish the motorist's capacity to attend to traffic and road conditions as well as induce him to make gross errors in judgment.

Persons employed in driving buses and trucks are aware that driving is hard work. The need to be constantly alert, due to the multitude of situations which can be encountered on the road, requires continuous concentration. After being on the road for a number of hours, the driver's eyes begin to tire and burn. His ability to react is blunted, and he tends to daydream. This happens even to experienced drivers who are in excellent physical condition, get plenty of sleep, and know when to take breaks. If this is the case, one can imagine what can happen to a person who is fatigued or under the influence of alcohol or drugs.

Statistics bear out the fact that alcohol causes drivers to kill themselves and other motorists. Presently a large-scale campaign is going on to remove people from the road who drink and drive. However, fatigue is not as concrete a physical condition as drunkenness or the "high" caused by drugs. Law enforcement agents can pull over a swerving car, give the driver a test, and determine whether he has taken an amount of alcohol sufficient to impair his driving. Yet a state patrolman could not pull someone over and give him a summons for driving while fatigued. The onus is put on the driver himself to pull off to the side when he starts to feel tired.

Every effort must be made by enforcement and safety departments to indoctrinate motorists through signs and in driving courses that the mature thing to do when beginning to feel tired is to pull over for a short break and have something to drink that will help one keep alert. By emphasizing the role of maturity, these safety principles might become accepted more quickly by motorists, since people are usually attracted to the adult image.

Another factor which affects the individual's ability to drive is age. Some of the older drivers on the road today do not have sufficient reaction capabilities to be considered safe in all situations. However, to prevent someone from driving because of age is a sensitive and complicated issue, especially since individuals of the same age differ in ability—sometimes even radically. A number of motor vehicle bureaus are getting around this problem by administering annual or biennial driving tests to people 65 years of age or older. By doing this they are allowing for individual differences, because as long as some-one can pass the test—no matter what his age—he can continue to drive.

Hunger may also affect the motorist's driving. If a person is hungry, he will tend to become irritated more easily and drive faster. Also, it will tend to increase his tendency to let down his guard as he gets closer to home, thus making him more accident-prone.

A deficiency in vision is another physical determinant which could cause traffic accidents. For example, many people suffer from a form of color blindness, the most common variety being the red-green type. Persons with this condition have difficulty distinguishing green from red. Both colors appear yellowish to them.

Of this group, there are persons who are more insensitive to red than green. This condition is called *protanopia*. They need an extremely large amount of red to discriminate.

Deuteranopia, on the other hand, is a color-blind condition of the red-green variety in which the person with the defect is relatively insensitive to green.

The above physical problems are also affected by the existence of the phenomenon called the *Purkinje shift*. This phenomenon refers to the change in relative brightness between red and green under different levels of illumination. Green appears much brighter than red under dim illumination. (This phenomenon holds for the person with normal vision and should not be confused with the abnormal conditions of protanopia and deuteranopia.)

Insufficient time for darkness adaptation is a further example of a physical problem which can result in an accident. When it becomes dark, time is needed for the pupils to dilate so more light can be admitted. During such times of dim illumination, the rods of the eyes, which are responsible for night and twilight vision, become very sensitive. And so, if there is not enough time for the pupils to dilate, as in the case of the motorist who exits quickly from a properly lighted highway to a dark service road, the person will find it difficult to see the road ahead.

Or, if a person has a condition which has affected the periphery of his eyes, where the rods are located, he might have great difficulty seeing at night and should not be allowed to drive under such circumstances.

There are a number of physical conditions which might affect an individual's ability to drive safely. However, physical problems are obviously not the only factors in the cause of accidents. There are psychological ones as well.

The Insecure and Immature Motorist

Insecurity and immaturity in an adult are often manifested in the person's driving habits. If an individual tends to be childish and unsure of himself, he tries to overcompensate for his personal deficiencies by asserting himself behind the wheel. While in his vehicle, the insecure person may feel that other people cannot get at him because he's locked in by a barrier of steel and speed. To him driving appears to be the ideal activity in which to prove to others that he is truly powerful.

This attitude can also apply to the immature driver. He believes that through daring, fancy driving he will make a name for himself with his girl and his buddies. Both insecure and immature motorists therefore are often prey to exhibitionistic behavior while on the road. This exhibitionism takes the form of a demonstration of power in which they speed without consideration for safety, display foolhardy shows of "talent" by driving in a daring manner, and demonstrate "superiority" by tailgating and racing.

The only way the law can deal with these individuals is to take away their licenses until they become mature enough to drive like adults. In some cases this time may never materialize, and they will continue to lose their licenses or eventually reach a fatal end.

The Motorist's Intellectual Ability

Each person is unique because of his personality as well as his intelligence. Having examined some of the problems that can arise from a motorist's *personality*, we now look at the difficulties that may stem from his *intellectual ability* (or the lack of it).

Most states give written tests and a road test to potential operators of motor vehicles. They are designed to check the applicant's ability to understand the traffic regulations and to see whether he can perform a minimum of required maneuvers with a vehicle safely and efficiently. Ideally these tests should screen out people who do not have the aptitude or the training to be on the road. However, because of individual human differences this does not always happen.

Since different people make up the tests for the different states, the tests are not equally difficult. Since there are a large and varied number of examiners who administer the road test, and since they are subject to their own standards and emotions, their scoring is far from objective. Combine these two points with the fact that driving conditions vary from state to state, and one can see the problem involved in standardizing driving tests.

To illustrate, two extreme examples will be given. In San Francisco an intelligent individual who has taken a driver education course in the city applies for and receives his learner's permit. He goes to take the road test portion of the motor vehicle exam and is assigned to a rater who doesn't like the way he looks and fails him on some technicality. In another instance a person from a rural area takes and passes the written portion of the test on his fifth attempt. After this he is administered the performance sections of the exam in a small town. He passes, because of the lack of difficult situations present in the area to truly test the driver's abilities.

Now in the first case, the driver from the large city was not given a license even though he may well have been qualified, whereas the second driver was given one because he had the ability to drive well under local conditions. The problem is obvious. Of course, the first individual will eventually get his license, and with what he has learned he can probably drive well under most normal conditions. However, the second person, though he might not endanger anyone if he drives only in his hometown area, could endanger himself and others if he drives a distance to a large city using superhighways.

What's the answer? It's hard to tell. States have standardized the written tests, but the individual raters will never be objective on the performance part of the exam. It's just humanly impossible! The problem at this time is still under study in the effort to come up with a viable solution in the near future.

Inattention while behind the Wheel

A beautiful day, crashing surf, the changing of the seasons in New England—the countryside is full of beautiful sights. Unfortunately these attractions can lead to death for the driver who gazes upon them. Inattention to signs because of distractions inside the car or outside the window sometimes causes the normally careful driver to have an accident.

In a small Western town a man who felt himself to be a careful driver (he hadn't received a traffic summons in his twenty-four years as a motorist) was easing through the main street at 35 miles per hour. He was so taken up with the different shops that lined the street that he missed the sign saying "SLOW—20 mph—CHILDREN AT PLAY." A few seconds later a child darted out into the street from between parked cars. He couldn't stop in time, and the child was killed. The skid marks were measured afterwards; it was estimated that if he had been going at 20 miles per hour he might have been able to stop in time, and the sad story wouldn't have had to appear in the town's newspaper the next day.

In another case, a businessman from a large metropolitan city on the East Coast decided to take his family for a quiet drive in the country. As he got up into the Catskill Mountains, he started to notice the thick foliage in the hills above a dirt road which ran off from the highway. He turned down the narrow road to get a better look at the scenery. His wife suggested they get out and walk awhile, because the road seemed quite pitted, and he could take a closer look on foot. The man refused.

As they drove along, he got quite engrossed in the scenery. He didn't notice the dip in the road which was followed by a sharp curve. The car swerved. Luckily no one was hurt, even though the car was almost completely destroyed. It was another accident that could have been avoided if the driver had paid attention to his driving. It's no wonder that car insurance is so high in tourist areas. People who don't give their full attention to driving are a menace to those who care about life.

Driving and False Security

Just as one's body can be lulled to sleep when driving, one's mind can begin slumbering too in certain situations which cause the driver to have a false sense of security. Three conditions which are particularly responsible for this are:

1. Country driving
2. Highway driving
3. Driving on a cloudy day

Country driving is, on the whole, quite pleasant. There is less traffic on rural roads, and the only thing one has to worry about is "a stray cow or horse." Since the weather somehow seems pleasanter and the air is actually less polluted than in the city, the motorist tends to be more at ease behind the wheel. And because the occasion for many people to be in the country is a happy one, the driver is often in a good frame of mind. Driving in the country can give the motorist a sense of calmness and security. This is attested to by the fact that taking a nice, quiet drive in the country is a favorite old pastime.

The problem comes about when a city dweller leaves the country and returns to a bustling urban area. In place of the stray cow there is now a street full of people and rushing vehicles and overpowering trucks. In this situation the secure feeling of the country is no longer justified. If it is still felt by the driver, it is now a false security due to the presence of new challenges to his motoring skills.

Similar to this problem is the transition from highway driving to traveling on local thoroughfares. After driving for a period of time on roads which have no cross streets, stop signs, or traffic lights, it is difficult for the motorist to alter his frame of reference to take into consideration the many other factors not present on highways or expressways. Accidents are therefore quite common at the bottom of exit ramps and within several blocks of where a highway ends.

A third situation which causes false security occurs on a cloudy day. In this type of weather the streets are dry, and no sun is out to glare in the driver's eyes. As a result, no particular problem is present to make the driver wary. However, as is likely on a cloudy day, it begins to rain. Since the motorist has been traveling without incident up to this point, he tends not to consider the wet conditions.

This fact can be borne out by observing what happens in heavy rainstorms on large highways. Instead of slowing down, many drivers appear to speed up to pass those who have common sense and have slowed down due to the dangerous weather conditions. In some instances the motorist who is speeding along will not even realize what he is doing until it comes time to stop for a tollbooth; he applies the brakes, skids, and causes a pile-up which stalls traffic for miles.

False security is the cause of many avoidable accidents. In a driver safety course this subject should be treated properly so that the new generation of drivers being introduced to the road will have more respect for it than those driving today.

TWO EFFICIENT WAYS OF ENFORCING TRAFFIC REGULATIONS AND SAVING LIVES

Periodic reinforcement and *conspicuous enforcement* are two useful methods to use in discouraging reckless driving and helping prevent driving fatalities. Both principles are in wide use today. It would be beneficial to see why these simple techniques are effective and when one method would be more suitable than the other.

Periodic or partial reinforcement is a method in which reward or punishment is not given every time in response to a particular action. This can be contrasted with continuous reinforcement, in which reward or punishment is administered 100 percent of the time in response to a particular action. An example of periodic reinforcement is seen in its use as a reason for an individual's telling jokes. People don't laugh at them all the time but find them funny on occasion. Since the joke teller has had success in the past, he is prompted to continue the behavior in the future, even though he knows there is a chance that people might not laugh. Punishment can also be administered on a partial basis, as is shown in raising children. Youngsters are caught doing naughty things on *some* occasions only and are physically reprimanded only some of the time.

Of the two forms of periodic reinforcement and continuous enforcement, the latter is more effective. However, periodic reinforcement is more practical to use in law enforcement. If a man is traveling along a particular two-mile strip of highway on a regular basis and becomes familiar with it, he may tend to speed after a while because he believes that he knows it well enough to chance the extra acceleration. If there were a patrolman stationed at every half-mile interval, he wouldn't be able to speed.

This example illustrates aptly how state patrol departments can use periodic reinforcement. Ideally, then, almost the same good results can be obtained with fewer men on the highways as long as the attitude that "the police are everywhere" becomes prevalent in the minds of would-be violators.

In addition, in the case where periodic reinforcement is used instead of continuous reinforcement, it appears that motorists will not revert to the undesirable behavior as quickly when the reinforcement is removed. In other words, if there is a road which a patrolman is always assigned to monitor and he is removed, the motorist will become aware of this and may start to speed again. However, if there is a road where a patrolman is only sometimes assigned, the motorist will be less likely to speed, feeling that there is still some chance he may be around today even though he wasn't there yesterday. As a result, periodic reinforcement is an ideal principle to employ in enforcing traffic regulations.

Conspicuous enforcement was the other technique mentioned which can be used to discourage reckless driving. By conspicuous enforcement is simply meant the stationing of a police car or some substitute (such as radar signs) in places where a driver can plainly see that a peace officer is somewhere in the area. Observing this usually makes him obey the traffic laws faithfully. This method is accomplished by assigning roving patrol cars, stationing clearly marked police vehicles along the road or on the mall where they can be seen easily, and having a high concentration of radar traps.

Whereas the previous technique is used to encourage compliance with traffic laws and is a long-range method used to bring about good driving behavior, conspicuous enforcement is a direct approach to saving lives. When a patrol car is posted with its lights blinking near a school zone, the goal is not to catch speeders but to force motorists to slow down so that they won't hit a child crossing the street. This also applies to densely populated areas and in places where a sports or cultural event is being held. In these instances the immediate goal is to save lives. The time of year also dictates when conspicuous enforcement is best utilized. Memorial Day and Fourth of July weekends are examples of times when the roads are especially dangerous to travel.

Both periodic reinforcement and conspicuous enforcement can be useful to traffic enforcement departments and have particular situations in which they can most appropriately be used. Both methods are based on psychological principles and are further evidence for those who believe that studying psychology is useful for law enforcement officers. Psychology can be an aid in understanding why people are doing certain things today as well as an aid in developing new and effective methods for tomorrow.

HOW VIOLATORS SHOULD BE HANDLED

In dealing effectively with traffic violators three questions that the officer must ask himself and answer correctly are:

1. Who is the traffic violator?
2. Whom and what do I represent?
3. What is my job?

The first question does not mean "What is the motorist's occupation? " or "What is his name? " It means that we must realize that the traffic violator, in most cases, is not a criminal, but a negligent fellow-citizen. Of course, when an officer pulls someone over he must be prepared for anything; there is always the possibility that the motorist may be a criminal as well as a traffic violator. However, for the most part, those who speed or drive carelessly are citizens who have used poor judgment on this occasion.

With this in mind it is very important that in response to the second question, whom and what do I represent, the officer also knows the proper answer. For the average individual, the traffic patrolman is one of the few contacts he will have with a law enforcement agency and probably the only one he will have with an arm of the nation's system of justice.

How the officer handles the encounter determines the image of the local police force, the city, and the state. This point is not far-fetched. When a New York, Alabama, or another state highway patrolman steps out of his car, he represents the state which employs him, just as the reader of this book represents his city or state. If this fact is forgotten, the department and the area image can be hurt immeasurably.

The third question was "What is my job?" As suggested in the previous paragraph, the patrolman's position requires that he represent his state by conducting himself professionally in a courteous, serious, and dedicated manner. Still, there is one other role he should perform in order to be thorough—the role of an instructor in driver safety out in the field. There are many instances where this function is necessary.

A prime example is the situation when an individual jumps the stop sign or red light because no one appears to be coming the other way and then complains when he receives a ticket. He must be informed that if he and other drivers break the habit of stopping on signal, they may inadvertently make a slip in the future, pass through a stop sign or red light, and meet a fatal end. Often a driving safety lecture doesn't get through to motorists, but a ticket and a logical explanation by an officer on the scene does.

To review, then, the traffic officer should be able to answer correctly to himself three questions: (1) Who is the traffic violator? (2) Whom and what do I represent? and (3) What is my job? A proper understanding of these questions can result in making the officer more efficient, courteous, and professional in the performance of his duty.

One final comment on handling the traffic violator should be included before leaving this area: namely, how to handle the person who is irate about receiving a ticket.

When dealing with an angry motorist, the officer, being in a position of authority, is often tempted to react in a strong verbal manner to what the person says. Yet doing this could cause greater difficulty for both the officer and the motorist. The officer should try to allow the motorist to express himself within reason.

If the officer finds himself getting angry and unable to control himself because of the violator's attitude, he should not confront the person. Instead, he should walk around to another section of the vehicle to complete the summons or move away from him entirely once it has been issued. This is to allow his anger, which has reached a pitch, to dissipate; for if the officer loses his temper, he may overreact and be sorry for it later.

SOME ESSENTIAL ELEMENTS IN DESIGNING HIGHWAYS AND DEVELOPING ROAD SIGNS

The design of road signs is particularly important. Quick recognition of directions to slow down, prepare for a curve, or be aware of a special road condition ahead is necessary if accidents are to be prevented. In addition, improper marking of signs can cause confusion which may lead to frustration, thus upsetting the driver and adversely affecting his ability to make a cool, calm decision. Furthermore, signs which are inadequate because they are faded, distorted, or too small require the motorist to pay extra attention to them. This effort serves to increase the strain on his eyes and can lead to sleepiness or eventual inattention to the road indicators.

With these problems in mind, highway engineers and other staff specialists make every effort to create signs which are extremely easy to recognize in plenty of time to make the required judgments. This is accomplished by letting the sign's shape, size, lettering, and color assist the motorist in understanding the directions being given. The shape of a stop sign is different from that of a "yield" indicator; a railroad crossing marker is distinguishable from one which gives the motorist directions.

Size is another factor which helps. In many areas the stop signs are deliberately made particularly large so that they can be seen from a distance and the motorist can slow down accordingly. However, the most basic recent advance has been in the lettering of signs. Today most information is printed on a background with reflecting letters that are raised. Written traffic instructions are more legible now than ever before and stand out extremely well, even at night, because of the type of coloring and lettering used.

Added to the three sign techniques above (shape, size, and lettering), color has always been a method of giving information. Red means danger and yellow indicates caution to drivers all over the country. This standard color system has proved very effective in traffic control.

To recapitulate, signs have been improved to date and will continue to be studied for future development. If they are confusing or illegible, they are downright dangerous. It is not surprising, therefore, that sign testing and design has become such an essential area of study for the department of highways in each state.

Hypnosis from driving has been with us for a long time. For years, tired motorists have been lulled to their death by staring at the little white line in the middle of the road. With the construction of long, level, straight superhighways this problem has become even worse. Highways have often become so uniform that even in daylight hours they have a hypnotic effect.

Highway engineers have taken a few steps to offset this growing difficulty. These efforts include making roads more interesting, livelier, and even to some extent, more challenging. Roads are being designed today purposely with gradual curves in them to require the driver to pay attention to what he's doing. Also, blinking signs that carry the simple message "Stay awake" have been installed on many thoroughfares. These techniques (blinking signs and roads designed to require the driver's attention) are only a few token measures taken by engineers and safety officials today in an effort to prevent road hypnosis. As in the case of sign development, they are still looking for better ways to aid in accident prevention through engineering.

DRIVER EDUCATION

Driver education is one of the most effective and widespread approaches to the traffic problem today. New motorists are getting an extra lease on life by attending professionally prepared lectures on safe motoring.

Often law enforcement officers are asked to instruct classes in this area, so it might be helpful if three points were covered to assist officers in the event that they are called upon to give a lecture. The three points are:

1. Attitude of the instructor
2. Use of "shock" movies
3. Driving and education

The first thing to note is that the instructor's attitude can influence the whole impact of the class. If he is convinced that the subject of traffic safety is an important area and one that should be spoken about whenever the opportunity presents itself, he will be able to create the right kind of atmosphere. Too many instructors in driver education leave the impression that they are being forced to teach it or are doing it for the money. This kind of outlook can do harm rather than good for the students in the class.

The use of "shock" movies has always been a favorite technique in driver education lectures. However, at this time they have almost outgrown their use. If excellently prepared and shown only once to the audience, shock movies can be a fine training aid. Yet due to the fact that almost all instruction in the area of safety includes such a film, most of the young have seen them already. Showing them more than once only serves to negate the effect they originally had. Furthermore, they can even become a source of ridicule if they aren't prepared well and are shown three or more times.

Driver education is just that—education. And this is how it must be viewed by an instructor. He should present the material seriously and with candor. The students have to realize that the subject they are listening to is a matter of life and death. They must recognize that safety on the roads is an adult area of interest. A mature presentation is therefore necessary for this to be achieved.

To sum up, the basic key and general rule for teaching driver education classes is to treat those whom one is addressing as adults by giving the lectures as an adult. It sounds simple, but—tragically enough—many lecturers in highway safety don't get the message across, and the groundwork is laid for future fatalities rather than sensible driving by tomorrow's motorists.

WHAT WAS COVERED IN THIS CHAPTER

Why people take chances on the road was treated by looking at the effects of the following six factors:

1. The mental state of the driver
2. The motorist's physical condition
3. The insecurity or immaturity of the driver
4. The motorist's intellectual ability
5. Inattention while behind the wheel
6. Driving and false security

Illustrations were given of how a motorist who was angry, depressed, frustrated, or elated might become involved in an accident because of his emotions. Fatigue, drugs and alcohol, hunger, age, and difficulties in vision were also cited as contributing causes of accidents.

Protanopia and deuteranopia, color-blind conditions of the red-green variety, the Purkinje shift, and the problem of darkness adaptation were among the perceptual difficulties noted. The inability to see the road ahead clearly when quickly moving from a lighted highway to a dark side road and problems encountered in seeing the red or green light under various conditions were shown to be possible in the presence of the above difficulties.

Country driving, traveling on a cloudy day, and highway driving were given as examples of situations which might foster feelings of false security in a motorist. For example, in country driving there is much less interference on the road to worry about. This could instill a sense of confidence in the driver to the extent that he might not appreciate the change in the driving demands when he returned to the city.

Periodic reinforcement and conspicuous enforcement were shown to be two useful methods of saving lives and discouraging reckless driving. Moreover, illustrations of their use by law enforcement officers pointed to ways in which manpower can be saved when they are applied.

In handling traffic violators three questions were posed for the officer to ask himself:

1. Who is the traffic violator?
2. Whom and what do I represent?
3. What is my job?

Also, advice was given on handling an irate violator in order to prevent a difficult situation from resulting in an unfortunate emotional outburst.

In the brief examination of the topic of highway and sign designs, the danger of monotonous or confusing roads was noted, along with the usefulness of color and shape as other factors in transmitting road information.

This chapter was designed to introduce the officer to several basic areas in traffic control and safety. Since traffic safety is, in fact, a matter of life and death, this topic is obviously one of great importance. The basics presented here should serve as a stepping-off point to more advanced studies provided by texts and periodicals devoted primarily to traffic safety.

REVIEW

1. What were the six factors covered in this chapter which may cause motorists to speed or drive recklessly?
2. What is the difference between protanopia and deuteranopia?
3. What is the Purkinje shift?
4. Give three examples of situations which might foster false security in a motorist.

5. What are two efficient ways of enforcing traffic regulations and saving lives? Give an illustration for each of them.

6. In dealing with traffic violators who are becoming angry or offensive, what should the officer do to prevent the situation from getting unnecessarily worse?

7. Apart from the lettering, what are two other ways in which traffic signs give the motorist information?

8. How useful are "shock" movies in a driver education program?

chapter thirteen

Crowd Control in the Street and in the Correctional Facility

Aggression on the part of a single individual can result in a significant loss of life and property, but group violence can end in a disaster impressive enough to shake an entire nation.

> Violence cannot build a better society. Disruption and disorder nourish repression, not justice. They strike at the freedom of every citizen. The community cannot—it will not—tolerate coercion and mob rule.
>
> Violence and destruction must be ended—in the streets of the ghetto and in the lives of people.[1]

Yet knowing that mass disruption is intolerable and promising to attack the problem are obviously not the same as solving it. Unfortunately there is no simple solution available which, if applied, would prevent the occurrence of large-scale civil disobedience. As pointed out in a recent government study, the methods used in the past might not even be applicable today.

> City law enforcement officials and other authorities can no longer rely on "leaders" in the Negro community to keep them informed of potential explosiveness in the ghetto. They need

[1] *Report of the National Advisory Commission on Civil Disorders* (*New York Times Edition*), E. P. Dutton, New York, 1968, p. 2.

objective data on what level of grievances exists so appropriate action can be taken to relieve tension.[2]

Today crowd control in the street and in the correctional facility is primarily in the hands of the individual officer. How he handles an incident may well determine the extent of the violent effects.

CROWD CONTROL IN THE STREETS

CROWDS

Not every group is a crowd, not every crowd is a mob. A group is merely an aggregate of individuals, whereas a crowd is a group which has been tentatively bonded together. They may be joined by an interest in an automobile accident or by a desire to attend a particular movie or perform a specific act, such as dancing. Crowds generally are neither organized nor unruly.

Handling crowds usually presents no problem if:

1. Some show of police force is evident.
2. Proper leadership and orderly traffic procedures are utilized.
3. Harsh control is not imposed on normally acceptable emotional outlets.

Ignorance of the third point often contributes to difficulties in crowd control. Officers who realize that crowds have no leaders and should therefore be guided properly to avoid a takeover by an irresponsible person may apply too many improper controls on a harmless crowd. To a group of laughing, slightly inebriated youths, unnecessarily harsh words by the police might have the same effect as the announcement at a baseball game that the fans were forbidden to shout and cheer. Though law enforcement officers should be alert to destructive venting of hostility, they must take care not to step in on harmless expressions of feelings. To do so would be analogous to cutting off the normal route of escape of steam from a boiler. The result in both cases could be explosive.

CHARACTERISTICS OF A MOB

A mob, by contrast, is more cohesive, more purposeful, and therefore more potentially dangerous than a crowd. Law enforcement

[2] Blair Justice (Project Director), *Detection of Potential Community Violence*, Office of Law Enforcement, U.S. Department of Justice, Washington, 1968, p. v.

officers should be aware of some of the factors accounting for a
mob's formation and its subsequent actions.

A mob forms for many of the same reasons as a crowd, but in its
early stages the members of the group become bound more closely.
They receive strength, freedom to act out, and a sense of belonging
from the numbers around them.

In a mob the officer can expect to come into contact with varied
types of individuals, including the mentally ill, the criminal element,
and professional agitators as well as impulsive youths and "average"
citizens. Though the impulsive and criminal elements can wreak great
havoc and inflict terrible personal harm, the agitator is probably the
most dangerous mob member.

The agitator triggers mob violence by empathizing with the
feelings and current thinking of the mob, spreading half-truths, and
playing on the fears and aggressive instincts of the group. He will stir
up the mob in hopes of forcing the police to react violently and
become disorganized so that the mob can overcome them.

MOB FORMATION

Certain elements must be present before a crowd will develop into a
mob. The most essential of these elements are (1) cohesiveness, (2) a
central, common purpose, (3) high emotionality, and (4) leadership.

Mob potential begins to be actualized when the cohesion of a
crowd starts to seal. For this to occur, a central purpose or common
bond must be shown to exist for the mass of individuals present so
that uniqueness and individuality can be suppressed, group identification can be advanced, and a feeling of anonymous unity can result.
Often the catalyst in this process is an event outside the group.

A group may erupt dramatically into a volatile mob due to an
indiscriminate police shooting. More commonly, though, a mob
develops slowly and steadily in reaction to an actual or perceived
situation which affects most of those present.

After a group is either quickly or gradually firmed up by an
outside influence, it is then preconditioned for exploitation by a
leader. Leadership is needed to foster greater unity, increase emotionality, and encourage action. A leader may do this by moving
about in the crowd to inflate the self-image of the members who are
in overt sympathy with his beliefs. He may also repeat and emphasize
the needs of the mob and allude to the presence of a certain enemy
(the force he wishes them eventually to release their aggression
against).

Once the mob begins to respond to his efforts, the leader will seek
to channel the individuals into a position where antisocial actions
will seem desirable—almost heroic. One of the ways he accomplishes
this is by emphasizing the *we* and typifying the group as a whole as
an important representative of what is just and right. When this point
has been reached, the fiery crowd, incensed by perceived injustices
perpetrated against them, is ready to act. Under a cloak of group
anonymity, the members will act out their tensions as soon as any
excuse is presented to them, such as an "unjust" police action.

The police should therefore intervene prior to the stage at which
the leader has the mob members cohesive and emotionally keyed up,
if innocent people are to be saved from injury or possible death. The
innocent often include not only those whom a mob might act
against, but also a majority of the mob members themselves. Many a
law-abiding citizen is influenced to commit acts of group violence
because of factors present in the mob setting.

A person who is not normally prone to physical violence might
commit aggressive acts, even murder, when under group influence.
Some of the reasons for this are:

1. The sense of power numbers bring
2. The novelty of being involved
3. The opportunity to release pent-up emotions
4. The pressure to conform to group ideals

RIOT WARNING SIGNS

There are some general warning signs which may alert the police to
potentially riotous trouble areas. These signs come to light when
loosely related groups begin to make visible their feelings and beliefs.
Riotous mobs often form around issues involving race, economics, or
power. These particular groups are always in evidence. However, the
stages of active militancy differ, so the officer must be aware of the
level which a group may have reached in order to facilitate timely
police action.

There are three progressive stages. The first is characterized by
formal or informal verbal action by the group to make their feelings
known. At this stage, a particularly extreme racist group might begin
spreading propaganda; a previously unknown cause might be vocally
proclaimed for the first time; or a juvenile gang might begin openly
taunting legal authorities and harassing local citizens.

The second level's onset is marked by the commencement of

action in line with the verbal beliefs expressed in the first stage. For a racist group it could mean arming themselves against their enemies. In the instance of the newly proclaimed followers of a cause (e.g., antiwar) it could be the start of organized marches, sit-ins, etc. And in the case of a juvenile gang, minor crimes would mark this second level.

The third and final level prior to all-out riot is the commission of significantly violent acts. These acts would be similar for most groups and would include those mentioned above. How imminent a riot might be could be determined by the number and magnitude of active hostilities.

MOB CONTROL

Timely, sensible action by the police is essential, then, if mob violence is to be thwarted. Such actions include:

1. Dispersing mobs in their initial formation stage
2. Instilling in responsible leaders and members a desire to control themselves
3. Recognizing and removing those who are responsible for increasing the problem
4. Containing the group within a specific area

In controlling a mob the individual officer becomes the man in the middle. He's influenced by the mob, his fellow officers, and the gravity of the situation. He may identify with the people he is trying to control if they happen to be of the same race or nationality or from the same part of the city. Yet he may at the same time be repelled by their verbal abuse, fearful of their mass strength, and resentful of what they seem to be planning to do.

The officer's coworkers also influence his feelings. Further confusion and concern may grow within the officer as he hears hatred and ideas about brutality expressed by some of the participants in one instant and sees the mob badly injure a friend in the next.

Tension may add to the officer's conflict and anxiety because he realizes the serious implications of his actions. Riots have been triggered by the overreaction of one officer; conversely, deaths of police officers have been attributed to indecision by one of their comrades.

Thus in riot control assignments the officer must not only be alert to the actions of the mob and his fellow officer, but he must also be aware of his own feelings. If an officer can remain calm, he should prove to be effective at the tense riot scene. To remain calm he must take the time to consider his own motivations as well as those of the other police officers and the members of the mob. His reactions ought to be in line with what is required of him and not cause him to display an unfortunate emotional response to a situation into which he has been baited by the mob.

Good mob control is based on dispersing people when they are initially forming large crowds in a particular area, removing persons who are increasing the tension, and instilling in receptive mob members a realization that they should follow the guidance of the law enforcement personnel. Yet control is centered even more on the individual officer's ability to remain calm and confident despite the hostility of the crowd and the effects of any other influences present at the time.

CROWD CONTROL IN THE CORRECTIONAL FACILITY

A prison riot. . . . Violence, injury, bloodshed, death—its horror can upset the most experienced correction officer, and its brutal outcome can shake even the toughest prisoner. A riot, a significant group disturbance started for a particular reason or reasons, may have a sudden beginning, but its occurrence usually need not be a surprise. Correctional personnel should be able to prevent or at least be alerted to it, since a riot has observable causes and warning signs. If a disturbance occurs in an institution with an alerted staff, it should be possible to limit the disturbance through use of proper methods of control.

RIOT CAUSES

Riots never really have only a single cause. Though a particular event may trigger (precipitate) a riot, other underlying (predisposing) causes must usually be present if a mass disturbance is to develop. Precipitating and predisposing causes can be attributed both to problems and to general as well as specific difficulties.

Obvious institutional failures often responsible for triggering riots are (1) bad food, (2) lack of meaningful work, (3) brutality, (4) inadequate recreational and educational facilities, and (5) harsh regulations.

Though obvious causes play a paramount role in causing riots, there are numerous institutional causes which are not as concrete. These somewhat vague factors are just as important (if not more so) as the tangible ones so easily observed by would-be prison reformers. Some of these major intangible predisposing factors can be grouped under the following basic headings:

1. Loss of human dignity
2. Frustration of natural freedom
3. Lack of personal stimulation

An inmate loses his sense of human dignity in a number of ways when he's incarcerated. The almost complete absence of responsible activities for the confinee to become involved in, the anonymity of being just another body to be checked during the daily prisoner counts, and the sexual degradation to which the inmate is often subjected are all elements accounting for the loss of his human dignity.

Frustration of natural freedom also causes pressure to build up inside the individual, adding to the degradation just mentioned. Confining a person to a limited area, with paramilitary regulations and schedules, and putting him in a situation where choices are not offered provides for a stressful environment.

The inherent lack of stimulation in prison life further predisposes the inmate to accept rioting as a sensible alternative. The bored, inactive inmate who is confined to a drab, depressing physical setting, occupied by monotonous tasks, and deprived of heterosexual activity may sink to a position in which any stimulation—even a violent one—would be viewed as acceptable.

In addition to the above, there are a number of factors which cannot be directly attributed to institutional problems. Some of them are:

1. Society's attitude toward corrections
2. The climate of modern life
3. Failures of the criminal justice system
4. Untreated personality disturbances in the criminal population

Society's apathy and ignorance concerning prisoner rehabilitation have adversely affected the growth of most penal systems. Lacking the support and guidance of an interested, enlightened community, correctional institution leaders have often emphasized security, resorted to physical brutality, and ignored any meaningful attempt at treatment.

In addition, society's growing unrest, as well as the confusion and tension produced by an antiquated, often unfair criminal justice system, further increases the inmate's anxiety and actually encourages him to deal with this anxiety by physical revolt. The situation is obviously serious, when one considers the type of person who is being pressured by all of the above factors. A significant portion of the prisoner population have notable psychological and economic problems. Many confinees:

1. Have an inadequate family background (see Chapter 5)
2. Are militant
3. Lack adequate education
4. Cannot control their impulses and act out in a violent manner even under *normal* stress
5. Are adolescents or immature adults

Clearly, the nature of the prison population is another predisposing cause which makes the correctional institution a powder keg ready for ignition by any of the precipitating causes mentioned earlier.

RIOT PREVENTION

Knowing the factors which contribute to the development of riots is only the first step. As shown in the previous section, riots are hard to prevent since many of the factors are beyond the control and treatment of the correction personnel. As a result, correction officers and their supervisors are limited in what they can do to prevent riots. However, two basic steps are within their power, which could possibly block a minor disturbance from spreading or prevent unacceptable conditions from being present at all. The two steps to be taken are:

1. Become familiar with the philosophy and operations of facilities which have successfully minimized riotous conditions.
2. Attain an awareness of the early warning signs of a planned disturbance.

In examining the philosophy of the progressive penal institutions, one can observe a number of effective measures which are in operation. Sometimes these measures are specific, sometimes they are generally accepted beliefs that are logical offshoots from the overall philosophy of the institution. Most of the varied techniques or beliefs can be included under one of the following general categories:

1. Effective communications
2. Fair treatment
3. Active, decisive leadership

Effective communications must exist between officers and supervisors as well as between inmates and officers. Though this is accepted, unfortunately it is rarely practiced. Inmates' comments are often met with ridicule and defensiveness by the correction officer. Ironically, the officer may receive the same type of treatment when discussing possible solutions to a problem with his superior. Unless the lines of communication are kept open, rumors will spread to make up for the missing flow of accurate information via accepted channels. Rumors are capable of causing mistrust and anxiety and of significantly blocking any access the correction personnel might normally have to the inmate population.

Other problems are the absence of treatment and the lack of active, decisive leadership on the part of the facility staff. Quite frequently there is unfair treatment in the form of harsh disciplinary measures, favoritism, and lack of adequate medical attention. Such unacceptable conditions produce tension which can be further increased by officers and administrators who ignore them. An officer who puts a prisoner on report when an infraction hasn't actually been committed and a deputy warden who is not consistent in determining the amount of punishment may inflame the unstable inmate population to their breaking point, resulting in a mass expression of aggression—a riot.

To prevent riots, all correction personnel should aid in furthering effective communications, fair treatment, and active, decisive leadership; the correction officer in particular should:

1. Be alert to those inmates who seem to be anxious to undercut the inmate-officer working relationship.
2. Seek to be impartial in the handling of all confinees. A favor done for one confinee can cause bitterness just as disciplinary inequities can.
3. Be professional in correcting an inmate. Verbal and physical abuse only enrages the prisoner and indicates to those present that the officer has a temper and may be trying to compensate for a lack of self-confidence.
4. Never threaten prisoners with a particular disciplinary action. Since the disciplinary board may not always provide the action which the officer on the tier thinks should be given, threats serve only to undermine the credibility of the officer.
5. Keep supervisors informed of problems and any possible signs of trouble.

6. Show interest in prisoner complaints, following up those that are legitimate.

WARNING SIGNS

Despite the correction officer's use of preventive measures, a disturbance or riot may occur. There are too many other factors not controlled by the individual officer to expect that his expertise will in all circumstances be able to forestall a riot. The officer must always be alert, so that if a riot or disturbance is being planned, he can pick up telltale signs.

Changes in routine inmate behavior usually provide the best warning signs. Examples of such alterations in behavior indicative of *well-planned* riots are:

1. Hoarding of commissary goods, particularly food
2. Disappearance of a significant amount of wooden and steel utensils, furniture, or their parts
3. An increase in the number of voluntary segregations coupled with a decrease in minor infractions by usual troublemakers
4. A decrease in usual communications between officers and normally friendly inmates
5. Elaborate homemade weapons found in a weekly search

There are instances where an impending disturbance may result due to general inmate dissatisfaction. In these cases—especially with youthful offenders—the warning signs may be quite different and more obvious, such as:

1. An increase in the physical violence perpetrated by inmates among themselves and on correction officers
2. A significant rise in the number and severity of institutional infractions
3. Frequent gathering of inmates
4. An unusual amount of complaints and bitterness outwardly expressed by large numbers of prisoners

CONTROLLING A RIOT

Naturally, just as it is essential to know some methods of action in preventing disturbances and to be alert to these warning signs, the correction officer must also be versed in riot control procedures. A potential disturbance can often be prevented, a small one contained, and a riot stopped when sensible measures are decisively taken.

Though specifics of control will not be covered here,[3] some general points regarding two topics will be made: the use of force and emotional contagion. *The use of force* in the quelling of a disturbance has always been a subject of debate. Though discussion still continues on what constitutes undue force, a number of things have become clear.

Often those correction officers guilty of using undue force when dealing with a minor inmate disturbance are *not* personnel assigned to the problem area but are from a mobile unit (e.g., transportation) which happens to be in the area. They may see a disturbance as an opportunity to act out their frustrations without fear of official reprisals, since it is possible for them to withdraw from the incident and the scene before the disorder is completely under control.

Undue force is sometimes welcomed by prisoners—unconsciously, if not consciously—so they can attract attention from outside the institution with the claim that they have been maltreated. This might be used as supportive evidence for the claim that in the past, too, they have been subjected to maltreatment. Even if this is not true, the current evidence of undue harshness adds credibility to their arguments which may be accepted by the public and the press.

Emotional contagion, in which the fever of emotion spreads from one person, group, or section of an institution to another, is another element that must be considered in riot control. If violence is isolated and curbed early, obviously further destruction can be greatly minimized. This is why a quick show of force and a quick identification and elimination of agitators are essential. The indecisive administrator and the hesitant officer are frequently responsible for the growth of a disturbance.

Just like riot prevention, control is primarily based on an attitude rather than on the size or number of clubs and other weapons the officers carry. If the inmate population believes that the personnel are informed, mature, confident, and fair, they will be deterred from creating a disturbance more than by the presence of physical deterrents. Fortunately, this fact is finally receiving acceptance today.

WHAT WAS COVERED IN THIS CHAPTER

Group violence in the streets and the correctional facility was discussed in this chapter. The organized, purposeful, agitated mob

[3] See the American Correctional Association's carefully prepared booklet *Riots and Disturbances in Correctional Institutions*, Chap. 3, for a comprehensive discussion of riot control.

was focused upon rather than the crowd. If a crowd is permitted to express itself through acceptable channels and is guided by police traffic control, it will usually remain unorganized and harmless. A mob needs closer attention and calm, confident treatment since characteristically its potential for violence is so great.

In the correctional facility, such obvious institutional failures as bad food, lack of meaningful work, brutality, inadequate recreational and educational facilities, and harsh regulations were cited as being only part of the cause for disturbances. Loss of human dignity, frustration of natural freedom, lack of personal stimulation, society's attitude toward corrections, the climate of modern life, general failure of the criminal justice system, and the nature of the prison population, though not as specific as the obvious precipitating causes, were also discussed because of the major role they play in causing riots.

Riot prevention was described in terms of two basic steps the officer should take if he wishes to aid in (1) eliminating institutional failures responsible for causing disturbances, and (2) preventing impending riots:

1. Become familiar with the philosophy and operations of facilities which have successfully minimized riotous conditions.
2. Attain an awareness of the early warning signs of a planned disturbance.

Control was then briefly viewed in terms of the use of force and emotional contagion. The point was made that control is primarily based on an attitude rather than on the size and number of clubs and other weapons. As always, use of weapons indicates a previous failure to instill a mutual respect between the inmate and the officer and a failure to eliminate the external apathy and ignorance in society which have produced inhumane conditions in correctional institutions. Now that society is beginning to open its eyes to the plight of criminal rehabilitation, the officer must also work to participate in corrections' new and progressive efforts.

Unless officers participate in such penal reform, riots will continue to increase, just as mass violence will continue to divide society in the street unless the police become part of the community again.

REVIEW

1. What is the essential difference between a crowd and a mob?
2. What are three general points to remember in dealing with crowds?

3. What are four sensible actions police can take to prevent mob violence?
4. List five obvious institutional failures often responsible for triggering riots in a correctional facility.
5. What are five psychological and socioeconomic problems of many members of the prison population which account for their predisposition toward violence?
6. List the warning signs of an impending riot in a correctional facility.

chapter fourteen

Community Relations and Law Enforcement

34 dead! Over 1,000 persons hurt! $40 million in property damages!

—approximate cost in lives and money of the Watts riots of August 1965.

We don't have the time! How can we afford to spend the money? Who needs a police-community relations campaign? What kind of business are we in, anyway—I thought our job was to lock 'em up, not coddle 'em.

— comment by a police officer from a major Eastern city in the United States.

SHOULD A LAW ENFORCEMENT AGENCY HAVE A COMMUNITY RELATIONS CAMPAIGN?

Over and over again the question is heard: "Why should we have a community relations campaign?" Some peace officers feel that time and money is wasted on any activity that is not directly and visibly

195

connected with crime prevention. Since the results of a community relations program are often intangible and its connection with law enforcement is indirect, it is sometimes considered to be useless.

However, this viewpoint is held by only a small number of law enforcement officers today. A community relations campaign which will enhance the understanding and cooperation of the public is generally seen as a necessary asset to the work of crime prevention.

> When Louisiana citizens refuse to cooperate with or participate in law enforcement the policeman's task moves from the formidable to the impossible.[1]

Proof of the above statement is very evident in modern times. In New York City policemen are being gunned down from behind. Just after the sun goes down, an officer who attempts an arrest in a large North Carolina city may find himself surrounded by local "citizens." Couple such occurrences with the everyday difficulties that indicate a gross lack of support for police activities, and the problem of citizen apathy becomes clear.

Though the problem of poor police–community relations is a mammoth one today, it did not grow up overnight. In order to create an atmosphere of understanding and mutual cooperation between the public and the police, the ugly passages of law enforcement history must be washed away. Television, movies, books, and the comments of those sensitive on the subject of human rights constantly remind everyone of past incidents of police brutality. Scenes are conjured up in which confessions are forced out of "innocent" suspects under harsh, glaring lights. Officers on the beat are caricatured as fat, corrupt, and unfeeling. The law enforcement officer is painted as a power-hungry individual who is not to be trusted.

This image is darkened further by the view the public has of police today. The policeman is no longer a human figure. The growth of cities and the inability of law enforcement departments to keep in step with population booms and physical urban expansion have resulted in the virtual elimination of the foot patrolman. A fleet of impersonal motor vehicles with menacing red lights has all but replaced the friendly, competent human guardian of the law who used to serve the local community. This situation is further complicated by charges of police brutality.

[1] Louisiana Commission on Law Enforcement and Administration of Criminal Justice, "Louisiana Crime Control Goals," pp. 11–12, May 1970.

An examination of seven riots in northern cities of the United States in 1964 reveals that each one was started over a police incident, just as the Los Angeles riot started with the arrest of Marquette Frye. In each of the 1964 riots, "police brutality" was an issue, as it was here, and, indeed, as it has been in riots and insurrections elsewhere in the world. The fact that this charge is repeatedly made must not go unnoticed, for there is a real danger that persistent criticism will reduce and perhaps destroy the effectiveness of law enforcement.[2]

For many of the citizens whom police officers serve and upon whom they depend for support, the present image of the peace officer is not what it should be.

The fact that those in law enforcement are fighting an uphill battle because of their present image and historical inadequacies in the field is not the entire problem. The situation is deteriorating because of the type of contact the average citizen has with the law. Cases in which the police are the "good guys" are very rare. How many times does an individual have his life saved by an officer? Not often. Yet, how many times has the average person been stopped and given a traffic citation?

In addition, if someone has had the misfortune to be robbed or mugged, the police sometimes become the target of the victim's emotions instead of a symbol of help. An hour after the crime has been committed, the person robbed wants to know why his valuables haven't been recovered. Just after he regains consciousness, a victim who was beaten and robbed while he lay drunk in a dark alley may be screaming at the very police who are trying to get some facts from him now that he's sober.

Indeed it is a somber situation. A good community relations campaign is far from the whole answer. It is only a beginning, a beginning that must be made to prevent the problems from getting worse. Progress in criminology and technology is truly on the move. It is now time to increase the pace of police–community relations because this area is just as important in the work of crime prevention as the more obvious areas of police responsibility.

Once a department has accepted the premise that a community relations campaign is needed, there remains the question of how such

[2] Governor's Commission on the Los Angeles Riot: *Violence in the City—An End or a Beginning?* Jeffries Banknote Company, Los Angeles, Calif., Dec. 2, 1965, p. 28.

a project should be conducted. The way this is answered could mean the difference between success and failure.

WHAT SHOULD BE INCLUDED IN A POLICE–COMMUNITY RELATIONS CAMPAIGN?

Community relations campaigns run by law enforcement departments can vary tremendously in size and detail. They can be dynamic, sophisticated, and well organized, or they can go almost unnoticed. Once a police chief from a small town was asked whether he had a community relations campaign. He asked what a community relations campaign was. When it was explained to him, his eyes lit up, and he said, "Sure we do!" When further questioned about how he conducted it, he explained, "Well, once a year we allow the local citizens to come in and see a display we have set up in the station house." So it is possible for community relations to be an extensive campaign or a once-a-year project. (However, it must be noted in defense of the the chief of police quoted above that he actually had an elaborate community relations campaign, but it wasn't spelled out. He often worked late hours to assist local residents personally. His rapport with the youth of the area was excellent, and he was always fair with those he protected.)

Community relations can be defined or undefined, formal or informal. With this point understood, we now turn to a number of principles that may be employed in a community relations campaign. Some of them are simply traits that might be stressed in training cadets. Others will be suggestions on what can be contained in a project designed to elicit public support.

No attempt will be made to cover the subject exhaustively or to list every suggestion which could be utilized to initiate or improve your department's community relations campaign. However, it is hoped that the following material will not only give the law enforcement officer concrete ideas but will also spur his interest and imagination to pursue further study and action in this area.

The topics which will be covered are:

1. Courtesy and maturity
2. Professional appearance
3. Education and community relations
4. Open communication and free dialogue
5. Elements of an organized police–community relations campaign.

COURTESY AND MATURITY:
BASIC TOOLS IN COMMUNITY RELATIONS

Be courteous. This almost sounds trite, yet courtesy is a forgotten art for a goodly number of law enforcement officers today. Unfortunately, however, it will always be the most basic tool in police–community relations. Why then is there a sizable minority of officers who aren't courteous? Perhaps there is a connection, in many instances, with insecurity.

The new officer often feels that if he doesn't exert himself at every possible opportunity, he will be in danger of losing the respect of the citizens he is assigned to protect. This also applies to the correction officer who is unsure of himself with the prisoners he's detailed to supervise.

An immature correction officer in a certain penal institution was always writing up inmates for disciplinary action for petty incidents. The result of this type of approach was not to instill respect for his position among the confinees but to create a weak image of himself. On one occasion he observed two inmates involved in horseplay. By simply saying "knock it off" the situation could have been rectified, and no further action would have been required. However, the inexperienced officer yelled, "You're on report!" Upon hearing this, the two confinees who were fooling around stopped smiling and turned angrily on the guard, and an unfortunate, unnecessary incident ensued.

This could easily have been prevented if maturity and courtesy had been employed by the officer. If he had realized that being firm with a prisoner does not require one to treat him in a discourteous manner, much unpleasantness could have been avoided.

Another area where courtesy is definitely required is that of telephone contact with the public. Most forces have a procedure for answering the phone, but even many of those who have a set policy still don't impress their officers with the fact that they must conduct themselves professionally throughout the entire phone conversation. An officer may answer the phone according to a standard operating procedure (e.g., "Twelfth Precinct, Sgt. Jones speaking"), but sometimes after this routine is completed, he forgets himself and can be heard saying things like, "Listen, lady, I've only got two hands."

It is understandable that an officer may lose his temper with an irate, irritating person on the phone. Yet it is essential for officers to realize that what they say on the phone may make an indelible impression on the caller concerning the efficiency and overall professionalism of the force. Some people's only contact with the police is via the phone, so courtesy should be an important element of police telephone procedures.

PROFESSIONAL APPEARANCE

In a major United States city recently, a government-employed bodyguard for foreign dignitaries had to work with the local police. His comment about them was, "They're sloppy!" He didn't mention whether they conducted themselves intelligently in the line of duty or praise their efficiency as effective, highly trained bodyguards. The only thing he said was in reference to their appearance. Offhand, the reader might feel as the author first did: Never mind how they looked, did they do their job well? However, after thinking about it for a while one can appreciate the importance of his appraisal.

How an officer looks makes an impression on those with whom he comes into contact. If his uniform is unbuttoned, his shoes are dirty, his stomach is sticking out, or he is unshaven and generally rumpled, he will "turn off" the young and lose the respect of the adults.

A uniform coupled with good personal grooming should enhance the position of law enforcement personnel. When the uniform is not kept with pride, it detracts from his appearance and injures the image of the entire department.

Holding daily inspections is one way to ensure that the men look acceptable. However, indoctrination on the purpose of good grooming is needed as well. Supervisors should be instructed that esprit de corps is enhanced by having a force that looks like a team of professionals. Individual officers should be taught that when they look the part of a peace officer, the actual performance of their duty will be made easier. The value of a good personal appearance cannot be overemphasized. Once a force begins to look sloppy, their work follows suit and becomes equally inadequate.

EDUCATION AND POLICE–COMMUNITY RELATIONS

Education is probably one of the most important elements in making the law enforcement officer more professional as well as more aware of the need for a community relations campaign. Certainly experience is irreplaceable, but education is a process in which one can reflect on what has happened in the past and profit from it. Education in psychology, for instance, helps the individual to achieve a better understanding of himself and the public with whom he must deal.

Being versed in the proper use of the English language as a result of taking college courses in communications serves to improve the officer's ability to make himself more clearly understood. Furthermore, in addition to general social science courses, there are a large number of police science courses which can directly help him in the performance of duty. Criminology, criminalistics, juvenile delinquency, corrections, civil law, and forensic science are only some of them.

Despite the value of education, it is still difficult to get some law enforcement officers to attend classes. Many of them feel that they have been away from school too long. Others do not believe they have the ability to do college work, even on the associate degree level. To this group can be added those who are lazy and those who can't afford the tuition.

These officers must be motivated to commence furthering their education and to continue once they have started. According to psychology, reinforcement is at the basis of motivation. Through simple applications of rewards, for example, continuing one's education can be made particularly desirable. Here are some techniques that may be used:

1. The cost of work-related courses can be absorbed by the department rather than the individual.
2. Educational requirements can be set for promotion to a particular rank (e.g., an associate degree for lieutenant).
3. Time off from work can be scheduled in order to enable the man to attend classes.
4. A professional library of magazines and books could be established at each station house.

These are only a few examples of rewards which could be offered to those who pursue their education. Any available technique must be used to motivate the members of your department to continue their schooling. If the program succeeds and most of the men do attend, the results will be amazing. Education can make peace officers better men and their departments significantly more professional.

OPEN COMMUNICATION AND FREE DIALOGUE

"He's really a mean-looking guy."

"He sure is, but you know, I've talked to him quite a few times, and he's as gentle as a lamb and seems to be quite easy-going."

The above fictional conversation reemphasizes a very important point that was made earlier in the book, namely, that people are not always as they seem. This concept is highly relevant to community relations. In a campaign to get the public and the police to work together, two basic facts must be emphasized, even if nothing else is achieved:

1. How a person talks or what color of skin he has does not determine what kind of person he is.
2. Because someone is wearing a peace officer's uniform, the local citizen need not consider him an alien.

If these points can be brought across to both the public and the police themselves, it will be a great step toward the much-needed unification of the two. Those in the law enforcement field are servants of the public; and in the prevention of crime, in the enforcement of the law, and in the correction of the criminal, public support is needed desperately.

The next task is to determine what steps a law enforcement agency can initiate to open the lines of communication between the public and the police. Indiana's Division of Parole, Department of Corrections, prescribes the following general approach in an annual report:[3]

> Our community relations will take on an even greater scope as we intensify our efforts to create community support through *public speaking and program participation.* [Italics supplied.]

These two techniques are ideal to increase the exposure of the force and increase the number of meetings the average citizen has with the police on an informal basis. Discussion groups, community action, and the holding of lectures can crack the ice that has formed between the man in uniform and his fellow citizens. During these artificial (and possibly forced) encounters, prejudices long enhanced by a lack of contact can often be lessened to the extent that more meaningful encounters will follow. Often people shy away from a new experience, but once they have been exposed to it, they become relaxed and enjoy it. In a sense, this is what community action attempts to accomplish.

[3] A. P. Tutsie, *Annual Report, Division of Parole,* Indianapolis, Ind., June 1970, p. 8.

As well as encouraging free dialogue between the public and the police, efforts should be made to open the lines of communication within the force. Law enforcement symposiums are ideal settings for this type of undertaking. If a symposium can be arranged in a relaxed atmosphere, with guest speakers followed by discussion groups, much can be achieved. Some of the possible accomplishments of this type of meeting would be:

1. The dissemination of up-to-date information in law enforcement
2. An opportunity to recreate and discuss problems with fellow workers in a nonthreatening atmosphere
3. Reinforcement of the idea that the men are professionals, which requires that they further their knowledge in their field

Such meetings with an educational or recreational purpose should have beneficial results and should indirectly improve the dialogue between, and teamwork of, the men on the force.

THREE BASIC ELEMENTS OF AN ORGANIZED POLICE–COMMUNITY RELATIONS CAMPAIGN

The three essential elements in a professional police–community relations campaign are:

1. The appointment and training of a qualified information officer-public relations director
2. The establishment of procedures to deal with citizen complaints
3. The formulation of a written plan to improve the image of the law enforcement officer.

In appointing someone to represent the department in place of the commissioner, certain traits should be sought in the candidates. They are:

1. Above-average intelligence
2. A college degree (if possible)
3. A good command of the English language
4. A likable personality
5. Minimum experience of four years
6. A strong, clear voice
7. Good posture and a healthy, well-groomed appearance

These traits are desirable because they will aid the officer in the public relations billet to be more acceptable to the public and the press, thus favorably enhancing the information he provides. How a person sounds and looks has a considerable impact on the formation of prejudices.

In this case, the public relations director wants to create a prejudice in favor of law enforcement officers and police policy rather than against them. Many an election has been won on the basis of appearance rather than ability. Therefore, great pains have to be taken to choose the right man for the job.

Once an individual is chosen, he must be properly trained to fulfill the functions of an information officer and public relations director. To expect him to perform well without formal training is foolish. A few dollars may be saved by having him learn from on-the-job training, but he will be less effective in the end. This method would take much more time, and in the process it might do irreparable damage to the department. It is advisable, therefore, for him to be sent for formal training in conducting press conferences, setting up static displays, and releasing news briefs.

Furthermore, once the right individual is correctly trained, his position must be properly established. In other words, a standard operating procedure should be drafted so that the limits of the office are defined. Then the department and the public must be made aware of its function. This is important because a vague, undefined program can make even the best public relations director ineffective.

Speaking of effectiveness, another essential element is the director's ability to be useful to the public. If he or his office cannot be reached in the evening hours when complaints occur, or if he has no access to the commissioner, he is useless. What purpose is served if his office is not open at night and he cannot handle a complaint expeditiously in order to avert an incident? And suppose he cannot take action on problems which he has encountered because he doesn't have access to those who make department policy? If situations like these arise, having a public relations director is a waste of time and money.

Care should be taken in the director's selection and training, then, and in addition when he fully assumes the position, he should be:

1. Always available
2. Able to advise and consult with the commissioner

The second basic element of any professionally organized police–community relations campaign is an established procedure to deal with citizen complaints. The public must feel that action will be taken on their problems. Moreover, the department must be geared to follow up any complaints, and this is a logical first step. Instruction on the use of a standard complaint form should be given during cadet training so that new police officers will be aware of the procedure even if they are not themselves involved in the actual processing of these forms.

The third element mentioned at the beginning of this section was the establishment of a written plan on how to improve the image of the law enforcement officer. Such a plan is necessary if the campaign is to be properly organized. Furthermore, once established, it can be used as a record of what actual goals were set and, in retrospect, how many of the proposed objectives were achieved.

GOALS OF A POLICE–COMMUNITY RELATIONS CAMPAIGN

Up to this point a number of techniques have been described which can make a police-community relations campaign more effective. Some general goals should be set up for the personnel involved in using them so that they will appreciate why they must expend certain efforts. A list of five general goals follows:

1. A public understanding of the police mission
2. An increase in the professionalism of law enforcement officers
3. Public acceptance of the personnel involved in keeping the peace and of their activities
4. Cooperation of all citizens with those involved in the field of law enforcement
5. Community respect for and pride in the police force

These goals should be set up for all the members of the department to strive for in their daily contacts with the public. If these ends are not achieved, but are nevertheless at least sought by those in the field of law enforcement, all is not lost; progress will be made. However, if they are abandoned, the friction between law enforcement officers and the public will steadily increase until there will be only one outcome—disaster.

WHAT WAS COVERED IN THIS CHAPTER

Effective community relations requires that the officer:

1. Act in a courteous and mature manner
2. Be aware of his personal appearance

3. Become involved in furthering his formal education and realize his part in community activities
4. Be willing to exchange dialogue freely with civilians in the community

Though the above steps are some of the ways in which the officer can improve relations with the community, they should not be thought of as the final solution. There are many other actions which could be initiated.

Moreover, regardless of how many steps are taken to improve community relations, police officers will still be subject to harassment and unprovoked attacks, even to assassination. Not that the efforts along the lines of community relations are a failure or a waste of time; rather, the above statement is made to remind the officer that, although community relations has an important purpose, it probably will never do away with the radical fringe. The purpose of community relations is not directed at converting radicals but at improving relations with the community as a whole.

The three basic elements of an organized community relations campaign are:

1. The appointment and training of a qualified information-public relations director
2. The establishment of a procedure to deal with citizen complaints
3. The formulation of a written plan on how to improve the image of the law enforcement officer

The above efforts are expended in order to achieve certain ends. Five goals of a campaign of the sort described in this chapter are:

1. A public understanding of the police mission
2. An increase in the professionalism of law enforcement officers
3. Public acceptance of the personnel involved in keeping the peace and of their activities
4. Cooperation of all citizens with those involved in the field of law enforcement
5. Community respect for and pride in the police force

More important than the presentation of specific goals or campaign elements, the primary objective of this chapter was to direct the officer's attention to the need for community relations and to give an indication of how such a project can be undertaken.

What law enforcement personnel do in the area of community

relations could very well determine the future course of their city or state. Only when each law enforcement officer and each citizen wakes up to the fact that he has certain responsibilities to his fellow human beings will the rioting stop and the nation be joined together again. It has to start somewhere. It must start with *you!*

REVIEW

1. Why is a police–community relations campaign necessary?
2. What is one of the primary techniques which can be used to lessen the prejudices between the police and the public?
3. List three basic elements of an organized police–community relations campaign.
4. List five goals of a police–community relations campaign.
5. Why is the time, money, and effort put into a community relations campaign worth it even if it may not affect those on the radical fringe?

appendix one

Periodicals of Interest to Law Enforcement and Correction Officers

American Journal of Correction. Issued bimonthly jointly by the American Correctional Association and the Bruce Publishing Company, 1821 University Avenue, Saint Paul, Minn. 55104.

American Sociological Review. Published bimonthly by the American Sociological Association, 1001 Connecticut Avenue, N.W., Washington, D.C. 20036.

Bulletin on Narcotics. Issued quarterly by the United Nations, Sales Section, New York, N.Y. 10017.

Correctional Research. Issued by the Massachusetts Correctional Association, 33 Mount Vernon Street, Boston, Mass. 02108.

Crime and Delinquency. Issued by the National Council on Crime and Delinquency, 44 East 23rd Street, New York, N.Y. 10010.

Crime and Delinquency Abstracts. Issued bimonthly by the Superintendent of Documents, U.S. Government Printing Office, Washington, D.C. 20402.

Crime and Delinquency Literature. Published six times annually by the National Council on Crime and Delinquency.

Criminologica. Published quarterly by the American Society of Criminology, Dept. of Sociology, Catholic University of America, Washington, D.C. 20017.

Criminologist. Issued quarterly by the Forensic Publishing Company, Ltd., 9 Old Bailey, London, E.C.4, England.

Criminology. Issued by the Department of Criminology and Corrections, Florida State University, Tallahassee, Fla. 32306.

FBI Law Enforcement Bulletin. Issued monthly by the FBI, U.S. Department of Justice, Washington, D.C. 20535.

FBI Uniform Crime Reports. Issued quarterly and annually by the FBI.

Federal Probation. Issued by *Federal Probation Quarterly*, Supreme Court Building, Washington, D.C. 20544.

Georgia Juvenile Association Newsletter. Issued by the Corrections Division, Institute of Government, University of Georgia, Athens, Ga. 30601.

INSCAPE. Issued by Southern Illinois University, Center for the Study of Crime, Delinquency and Corrections, Carbondale, Ill. 62901.

INTERPOL. Issued monthly by the General Secretariat, *Interpol*, 26 Rue Armengaud, 92 Saint Cloud, France.

Journal of Criminal Law, Criminology and Police Science. Issued quarterly by Williams and Wilkins Company, 428 E. Preston Street, Baltimore, Md. 21202.

Journal of Forensic Psychology. Issued annually by the International Academy of Forensic Psychology, Paul Quinn College, Waco, Tex.

Law and Order. Issued monthly by *Law and Order Magazine*, 72 West 45th Street, New York, N.Y. 10036.

National Sheriff. Issued bimonthly by the National Sheriffs' Association, Suite 209, 1250 Connecticut Avenue, Washington, D.C. 20036.

Police. Issued bimonthly by Charles C Thomas, Publisher, 302-327 East Lawrence Avenue, Springfield, Ill. 62703.

Police Chief. Issued monthly by the International Association of Police Chiefs, 1319 18th Street, N. W., Washington, D. C. 20036.

Police Journal. Issued monthly by Butterworth and Company, Ltd., 14 Curity Avenue, Toronto, Canada.

Prison Journal. Issued semiannually by the Pennsylvania Prison Society, Room 302, Social Service Building, 311 South Juniper Street, Philadelphia, Pa. 19107.

Probation. Published quarterly by the National Association of Probation Officers, 6 Endsleigh Street, London, W.C.1, England.

Social Problems. Issued quarterly; can be ordered from *Social Problems*, Business Office, P.O. 190, Kalamazoo, Mich. 49005.

Traffic and Digest Review. Issued monthly by the Traffic Institute, Northwestern University, 1804 Hinman Avenue, Evanston, Ill. 60204.

appendix two

Professional Associations of Interest to Law Enforcement and Correction Officers

American Correctional Association (ACA)
Woodridge Station
P.O. Box 10176
Washington, D.C. 20018

American Federation of Police (AFP)
1100 N.E. 125th Street
North Miami, Fla.

Americans for Effective Law Enforcement (AELE)
33 North Dearborn Street
Chicago, Ill. 60602

International Association of Chiefs of Police (IACP)
1319 18th Street, N.W.
Washington, D.C. 20036

International Conference of Police Associations (ICOPA)
1241 Pennsylvania Avenue, S.E.
Washington, D.C. 20003

International Footprint Association (IFA)
1095 Market Street
San Francisco, Calif. 94103

International Narcotic Enforcement Officers' Association (INEOA)
178 Washington Avenue
Albany, N.Y. 12210

National Council on Crime and Delinquency (NCCD)
44 East 23rd Street
New York, N.Y. 10010

National Police Officers' Association of America (NPOAA)
1890 S. Tamiami Trail
Venice, Fla. 33595

National Sheriffs' Association (NSA)
Suite 209, 1250 Connecticut Avenue
Washington, D.C. 20036

Society of Professional Investigators
Box 1107, Church Street Station
New York, N.Y. 10008

Selected
Bibliography

See Chap. 8, pp. 108–110, for Selected Bibliography on the Drug Problem.

Allport, G. W.: *Pattern and Growth in Personality*, Holt, Rinehart, New York, 1961.

American Correctional Association: *Manual of Correctional Standards*, American Correctional Association, Washington, D.C., 1966.

American Correctional Association: *Riots and Disturbances in Correctional Institutions*, Washington, D.C., 1970.

Arieti, S. (ed.): *American Handbook of Psychiatry*, Basic Books, Inc., Publishers, New York, 1959.

Aubry, Arthur S., Jr., and Rudolf R. Caputo: *Criminal Interrogation*, Charles C Thomas, Springfield, Ill., 1965.

Bard, Morton (project director), Law Enforcement Assistance Administration, National Institute of Law Enforcement and Criminal Justice, OLEA Grant No. 157: *Training Police as Specialists in Family Crisis Intervention*, U.S. Government Printing Office, 1970.

Benjamin, Alfred: *The Helping Interview*, Houghton Mifflin, Boston, 1969.

Bennett, James V.: "Prisons in Turmoil," *Federal Probation*, vol. 16, no. 3, p. 3, September 1952.

Brown, Claude: *Manchild in the Promised Land*, Signet Books, New York, 1966.

Buros, O. K. (ed.): *The Mental Measurement Yearbook* (6th ed.), Gryphon, Highland Park, N. J., 1965.

Buss, A. H.: *The Psychology of Aggression*, Wiley, New York, 1961.

Cabeen, C. W., and J. C. Coleman: "The Selection of Sex Offender Patients for Group Therapy," *International Journal of Group Psychotherapy*, vol. 12, no. 3, pp. 326-334, 1962.

Capote, Truman: *In Cold Blood*, Random House, New York, 1965.

Carroll, Charles R.: *Alcohol Use, Nonuse and Abuse*, William C. Brown, Dubuque, Iowa, 1970.

Coleman, James C.: *Abnormal Psychology and Modern Life* (4th ed.), Scott, Foresman, Glenville, Ill., 1972.

Correctional Association of New York and International Association of Police Chiefs: *Alcohol and Alcoholism: A Police Handbook*, Smithers Foundation, New York, 1965.

Cressey, Donald R., and David A. Ward: *Delinquency, Crime and Social Process*, Harper and Row, New York, 1969.

Earle, Howard H.: *Police Community Relations: A Crisis in Our Times*, Charles C Thomas, Springfield, Ill., 1970.

Eysenck, H. J. (ed.): *Handbook of Abnormal Psychology*, Basic Books, Inc., Publishers, New York, 1961.

Fenton, Norman: *An Introduction to Group Counseling in Correctional Service*, American Correctional Association, Washington, D.C., 1957.

Fincher, Cameron: *A Preface to Psychology*, Harper and Row, New York, 1964.

Fox, Bernard H., and James H. Fox (eds.): *Alcohol and Traffic Safety*, U.S. Department of Health, Education, and Welfare, Bethesda, Md., 1963.

Fox, Vernon: "Why Prisoners Riot," *Federal Probation*, vol. 35, no. 1, pp. 9-13, March 1971.

Gilmer, B. Von Haller: *Applied Psychology*, McGraw-Hill, New York, 1967.

Glasser, William: *Reality Therapy*, Harper and Row, New York, 1965.

Gordon, Raymond L.: *Interviewing Strategy, Techniques and Tactics*, Dorsey Press, Homewood, Ill., 1969.

Green, Hannah: *I Never Promised You a Rose Garden*, Signet Books, New York, 1964.

Guilford, J. P.: *Fundamental Statistics in Psychology and Education,* McGraw-Hill, New York, 1965.

Hartmann, Henry L.: "Interviewing Techniques in Probation and Parole," *Federal Probation,* March, June, September, and December, 1963.

Inbau, Fred E., and John E. Reid: *Criminal Interrogation and Confessions,* Williams and Wilkins, Baltimore, 1962.

Jackson, D. D. (ed.): *The Etiology of Schizophrenia,* Basic Books, Inc., Publishers, 1960.

Justice, Blair (project director), Law Enforcement Assistance Administration, Grant 207: *Detection of Potential Community Violence,* U.S. Government Printing Office, 1970.

Kaplan, Bert: *The Inner World of Mental Illness,* Harper and Row, New York, 1964.

Kimble, Gregory A., and Norman Garmezy: *Principles of General Psychology,* Ronald Press, New York, 1963.

Lindzey, Gardner, and Calvin S. Hall (eds.): *Theories of Personality: Primary Sources and Research,* Wiley, New York, 1968.

McCarthy, Raymond G. (ed.): *Alcohol Education for the Classroom and the Community,* McGraw-Hill, New York, 1964.

Matthews, Robert A., and Loyd W. Rowland: *How to Recognize and Handle Abnormal People: A Manual for the Police Officer,* National Association for Mental Health, New York, 1954.

Meehl, P. E.: *Clinical Versus Statistical Prediction,* University of Minnesota Press, Minneapolis, Minn., 1954.

Menninger, Karl: *The Crime of Punishment,* Viking Press, New York, 1968.

Miller, G. A.: *Psychology: The Science of Mental Life,* Harper and Row, New York, 1962.

Momboisse, Raymond M.: *Community Relations and Riot Prevention,* Charles C Thomas, Springfield, Ill., 1966.

_____ : *Riots, Revolts and Insurrections,* Charles C Thomas, Springfield, Ill., 1966.

Pacht, A. R., S. L. Hallech, and J. C. Ehrmann: "Diagnosis and Treatment of the Sex Offender: A Nine-year Study," *American Journal of Psychiatry,* vol. 118, pp. 802–808, 1962.

Pavlov, I. P.: *Conditioned Reflexes: An Investigation of the Psychological Activity of the Cerebral Cortex,* Oxford University Press, London, 1927.

President's Commission on Law Enforcement and Administration of Justice: *Task Force Report: Drunkenness*, U.S. Government Printing Office, 1967.

Radzenowicz, L. (ed.): *English Studies in Criminal Science, vol. 9: Sex Offenses*, Macmillan, London, 1957.

Report of the National Advisory Commission on Civil Disorders, New York Times edition, Dutton, New York, 1968.

Rogers, C. R.: *Client-centered Therapy*, Houghton Mifflin, Boston, 1951.

Shneedman, Edwin S., and Norman L. Forberow: *Clues to Suicide*, McGraw-Hill, New York, 1957.

Stumphauzer, Jerome S.: "Behavior Modification with Juvenile Delinquents: A Critical Review," *FCI Technical and Treatment Notes*, vol. 1, no. 2, 1970.

Smithers Foundation, Inc.: *Understanding Alcoholism*, Smithers, New York, 1968.

Sullivan, Harry Stack: *The Psychiatric Interview*, Norton, New York, 1954.

Sundberg, Norman D., and Leona E. Tyler: *Clinical Psychology*, Appleton-Century-Crofts, New York, 1962.

Terracuti, Franco, and Marvin E. Wolfgang: "The Prediction of Violent Behavior," *Correctional Psychiatry and Journal of Social Therapy*, vol. 10, no. 6, pp. 296–297, 1964.

Thomas, Piri: *Down These Mean Streets*, Signet Books, New York, 1965.

Toch, Hans: *Violent Men: An Inquiry into the Psychology of Violence*, Oldine, Chicago, 1969.

Tuteur, Werner: "Can Violent Behavior Be Predicted?", *Correctional Psychiatry and Journal of Social Therapy*, vol. 9, no. 1, p. 39, 1963.

Tyler, Leona E.: *The Psychology of Human Differences*, Appleton-Century-Crofts, New York, 1965.

_____ :*The Work of the Counselor*, Appleton-Century-Crofts, New York, 1961.

Wechsler, David: *The Measurement and Appraisal of Adult Intelligence*, Williams and Wilkins, Baltimore, 1958.

Wicks, Robert J., and Ernest H. Josephs, Jr.: *Practical Psychology of Leadership for Criminal Justice Officers: A Basic Programmed Text*, Charles C Thomas, Springfield, Ill., 1973.

_____, and _____: *Techniques in Interviewing for Law Enforcement and Corrections Personnel: A Programmed Text*, Charles C Thomas, Springfield, Ill., 1972.

Wilson, O. W.: *Police Administration*, McGraw-Hill, New York, 1963.

Wolfgang, Marvin E. (ed.): *Studies in Homicides*, Harper and Row, New York, 1967.

_____ : *Patterns in Criminal Homicide*, Wiley, New York, 1966.

World Health Organization: *Prevention of Suicide*, Public Health Papers, Geneva, 1968.

Index